Bright Light

Untold stories of the Top Secret War in Vietnam

Stephen Perry

Contact the Author

steve@perry.com

View photos of the people and places described in the book at

http://brightlight1968.com

<u>DEDICATION</u>

This book is dedicated to the military forces of the United States of America, especially to those left behind in the seething jungles of Vietnam. We must never allow their sacrifice to be in vain!

"You've never lived until you have almost died, for those who fight for it; life has a flavor that the protected will never know"
SOG Motto

"I am the light of the world, whoever follows me will have the light of life and will never walk in darkness."

Jesus Christ
John 8:12

The Boy Next Door

We all learned as children that the "Man of Steel", Superman was not really human at all. Our super hero was actually an alien born on the planet Krypton and sent to earth via a rocket ship by his scientist father. I can still clearly hear the announcement that Superman stood for "Truth, Justice and the American Way." This was something that I deemed important as a child and something that I would try to emulate as an adult.

What about America's real super heroes? Were they also "Strangers in a Strange Land" like Robert Heinlein's Michael Valentine Smith or maybe the sons of some fictional Rambo?

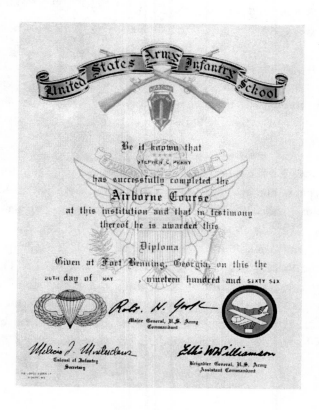

1

During my brief tour with the US Army I had the honor of standing and fighting beside many of those American super heroes. These real heroes were lads that sat next to you in church or who lived next door and perhaps mowed your lawn. These brave men had lived in our neighborhoods, attended our schools and churches and had done all the things that American kids do. But these brave men were different in a very special way. They too had the strong moral compass of Superman and had heard the call for "Truth, Justice and the American Way." They had heard the call of their country and had stood proudly to accept their responsibility as United States citizens. They were not afraid of the talk of war or its intrinsic dangers. These men volunteered over and over again for the good of their country. These men were the Green Berets of the Studies and Observation Group (SOG).

DONS BERET — Army Pvt. Stephen C. Perry, 20, son of Mr. and Mrs. George A. Perry, 6082 Dagny Circle, Huntington Beach, has become a member of the Green Berets upon completion of Special Forces training at Ft. Bragg, N.C. He will now be assigned to one of seven Special Forces groups around the world.

Green Berets were three time volunteers. First, they had to join the military on a voluntary basis and not be drafted. Secondly, they had to volunteer for airborne training and willingly jump out of perfectly good airplanes as part of that training. Thirdly, they had to volunteer for Special Forces. The volunteering part done, there was a long period of testing, qualifying and training before these young men could wear the Green Beret. Once awarded the beret, there remained a lot more training in a job specialty and in other areas such as jungle warfare and survival training. In the end, these few, these Green Berets, were the boys next door now grown into men of honor and dignity, highly trained and motivated to go wherever their Country would send them.

Special Forces medical class 67-1, Fort Bragg NC

My story began in Los Angeles, California where I was born to wonderful parents, George and Estelle Perry. My parents had dignity and had taught their children honor and love. My parents raised me as a Catholic. After moving to a home in Whittier, California in 1952, my sister Judy and I were enrolled in a Catholic grammar school named Saint Gregory the Great School. It was in St Gregory's parish that I learned more about my God and my Country. I learned that it was honorable to serve my Country and my God. I learned that the freedom to worship God was a right unique to free societies; and a right that was indeed worth fighting for.

Growing up I was a typical lad who enjoyed hiking, camping, nature, and the outdoors. I joined the Cub Scouts and remained a member of the Boy Scouts of America until I was fifteen years old. I made a number of the long - range hikes that were popular at the time including the Silver Moccasin and Golden Arrowhead hikes in the Angeles National Forest. I was "tapped out"(selected) for the Order of the Arrow when I was thirteen years old and I remember being taken out in the woods of the Brea Canyon by a young man dressed as an Indian brave and made to spend the night alone on the ground with no sleeping bag or tent. Little did I know at the time that I would repeat this act may times in the jungles of Vietnam.

One day at St Gregory's church I was saying the prayer that Roman Catholics say when they receive communion and I had a very special encounter with He who would remain my God and my protector to this very day. The prayer goes like this *"O Lord, I am not worthy that thou should come under my roof. Say but the word and my soul shall be healed."* I said the prayer devoutly while gazing upon the image of the crucified Christ hanging on the cross and I was overcome with a peace beyond my understanding. When the day ended, I got on with my youthful life and grew far from the God I had encountered that day.

I earned many badges and awards while I was a Boy Scout, but the best were the Ad Alteri Dei, the highest award a boy could earn from the Catholic Church, and the Rank of Eagle Scout, which is the highest rank a Boy Scout could earn. Not too many months after earning the rank of Eagle, my interest turned to hot rods, surfing and girls, and my days as a boy scout came to an end.

I graduated from St Gregory's in 1959 and attended high school at Don Bosco Technical Institute in South San Gabriel, California. I graduated from Bosco Tech in 1963 and attended my first year of college at what was then Fullerton Junior College (Now Cal State Fullerton). Since our family had grown over the years to now include my brothers David and John, and sisters Judy and Marilyn, it was time to replace our three bedroom house with one more suited to our family. A beautiful new five bedroom home was found in Huntington Beach and we moved in late in 1963. The following year I moved in with a few new friends from Orange Coast College. We shared apartments in Costa Mesa and later in Newport Beach where we lived until four of us enlisted in the Army in November of 1965. We enlisted on the buddy plan and each of us had hopes of winning the Green Beret.

I had enlisted with roommates Bert Merriman, Jim Sexton and Chris Cox. Each was just another "boy next door" until the spark of patriotism ignited a fire to serve. We all completed basic training at Fort Ord, California. We were tested and screened for Special Forces and two of us were selected to proceed to our goal. Friend Jim Sexton, the blond haired surfer I had shared many an adventure with while living on Newport Beach was found to be too young to proceed to Special Forces. At the time, a candidate had to be twenty one years old to begin training and since Jim would only be twenty, he was disqualified. Jim went on to serve out his years of enlistment somewhere in Alaska.

My friend Chris Cox was diagnosed with a severe case of asthma and was disqualified and later medically discharged from the service. Chris went on to become an entertainer. He moved to Aspen, Colorado and sang his ballads in clubs within the town over the years while he pursued his love of the mountains and skiing.

Bert Merriman and I were accepted for further qualification and training in Special Forces. We were sent to Fort Leonard wood, Missouri for training as combat engineers and from there to Jump school at Fort Benning, Georgia. After completing Airborne training and receiving our "silver wings," we were bused to Fort Bragg, North Carolina and the John F. Kennedy Center for Special Warfare. Here we were assigned to Special Forces (SF) Training Group where we were tested, screened, interviewed, and tested some more as part of the SF qualification process. After passing all the mental, physical and psychological tests we were given more tests to best determine our academic abilities and strengths. From here we completed eight weeks of Special Forces qualification training followed by issuance of our Berets and assignment to a Special Forces specialty school. Bert was sent to engineer school and I was sent to medical training.

For the next year I was trained in all aspects of medicine. My training was conducted at Fort Bragg, North Carolina and Fort Sam Houston, Texas and Fort Rucker Alabama. Classroom training was followed by on the job training at the Army hospital at Fort Rucker, Alabama. My medical training class got smaller over time as men failed to complete sections of the training. After completing on the job training we were returned to Ft. Bragg for another eight week class on tropical medicine and then the notorious "dog lab."

In dog lab we were assigned a patient (a stray dog collected from a local dog pound). My patient was ironically named "Whiskey" and, like my classmates, I became attached to my pet-patient. The patients were worked up medically and then one day each was taken into a chamber and shot through the meaty part of the rear thigh with a high-powered rifle. The high velocity of a bullet tearing through flesh sends out shock waves that kill flesh. Our job was to stop the bleeding, debride (cut out the dead tissue), and battle dress the wound. Over the following days and weeks we would change the dressing and nurse our patient back to health. When recovered, it was our job to put the patient under general anesthesia and amputate the leg as though it were a human patient. The patient was then over sedated and dog lab was complete. This whole process may seem cruel, but was necessary to give the Special Forces Medic the hands on training in skills that he would be expected to perform on his comrades when the need arose. Public protests at some point after my training led to a change where goats replaced man's best friend as the new patients of the SF medics.

After successful completion of dog lab, my surviving classmates and I stood individually before oral boards where we were tested orally on everything we had learned over our year of medical training. A team of four doctors fired difficult medical questions expecting correct and immediate responses to all. Several more of my classmates fell by the wayside as they failed to perform well under the pressure of the oral boards. By this time in the process, the men who washed out of the medical training were given the option to attend some other SF specialty training, but were not allowed to serve as Special Forces Medics.

After completing the Special Forces medical training there was another short training session of about eight weeks followed by graduation and assignments to the various Special Forces Groups around the world.

My friend Bert had graduated long before me due to the shorter nature of his training and he was already in Vietnam. Bert had been assigned to Project Delta. My classmates from my medical class (SF medical Class 67-1) were sent all over the world: Germany, Panama, Okinawa, and Vietnam; but I was left stateside, assigned to the Seventh Special Forces Group. My assigned duties for a time were to provide medical coverage for war games being conducted in the Smokey Mountains of North Carolina. It was here, in the then dry counties of North Carolina that I encountered my first moonshiners and sampled their potent brew.

Not wanting to be left behind, I called Mrs. Alexander at the Pentagon and volunteered again, this time for the Fifth Special Forces Group in Vietnam. Within a month, I received orders to report for transport to the Republic of South Vietnam. And so, the boy next door had become a man wearing the Green Beret.

After returning home for a two week leave I reported to Fort Lewis, Washington to be transported to the Republic of South Vietnam. It was here in early December of 1968 that I befriended Ken Cryan, another boy next door and native son of California. Ken and I became great friends and remained very close until his death in May of 1968. We traveled to Vietnam together, arriving at Cam Ranh Bay and from there to Fifth Special Forces Headquarters at Nha Trang. All of the other Special Forces men who had arrived with Ken and I were quickly assigned and shipped to their A or B teams around Vietnam(an A team was a basic twelve man special forces team while a B team was a larger support unit). Ken and I began wondering what was wrong with us that nobody wanted us assigned to their teams. Then one day before Christmas 1967, we were called into the office. As we stood at attention before the officers desk, the stoic faced captain informed us that we had both been assigned to C and C North, and that we had been held pending approval of our Top Secret Clearances. Neither Ken nor I had any idea of what the officer was talking about or what C and C North was. We were loaded on a C 130 transport later that day (Christmas Eve 1967) headed north to Da Nang, and by Christmas day, we had learned our fate as new guys assigned to the Special Operations Group (SOG). SOG was not officially part of the Special Forces operations in Southeast Asia, but Special Forces was used as a cover to shift highly trained insurgents into the top secret operations.

When Ken and I arrived at Phu Bai a few days after Christmas 1967, we stood formation with other newcomers and were greeted by the FOB 1 commander, Major Ira Snell. The Commanding Officer (CO) told us that the medics had a critical MOS (Military Occupation Specialty) and would be assigned to medical duties in support of the teams. He said that the FOB (Forward Occupational Base) was in dire need of volunteers to serve on the recon teams and that he would consider any of us who volunteered. After thinking about this overnight, I went to the COs office the following day and volunteered once again.

Major Snell was delighted with my choice and assigned me to ST Idaho under the command of SFC (Sergeant First Class) Glen Lane. In the following days and weeks, I would get to know the men on ST (Spike Team) Idaho during both training and leisure time.

Aerial View of SOG base FOB 1 (note zig zag trench lines)

Perfume River Ambush

The SOG recon teams trained continuously while not on actual missions. The teams practiced drills with hand signals until each man understood each of them and could take appropriate and immediate action when a signal was given. There were signals for almost every action needed in a combat situation and the team's stealth in carrying them out could mean the difference between life and death. The signals were first practiced in the FOB and as all team members became more proficient, they were practiced in the rice paddies and fields around the camp.

The team members were also trained on each of the weapons which could be carried on actual missions. The weapons included were the CAR-15, the M79 Grenade Launcher, the Colt 45, Browning 9mm and Walther PPK pistols. Training was also given on enemy and foreign weapons which were sometimes used on missions. The additional weapons training included the AK47, the Swedish K, the Sten gun, the Thompson sub machine gun and the UZI. Further training was also provided on the LAW (light antitank weapon), the M-60 machine gun and various explosives including the claymore mine, the M-14 "Toe Popper" mine and the use of C4 plastic explosives.

The training was sometimes monotonous or boring since it was repetitious for the already highly trained men of SOG. Things got more exciting when the teams would load up in the back of a deuce and a half (heavy two and one half ton truck), and head for the range. The range was just an open area with hills as a backdrop where the weapons could be fired without disrupting the quiet villages. On the range, no one would be endangered (except the team members who were firing the weapons). On one such day, one of the FOB's senior NCOs (Non Commissioned Officers) MSG (Master Sergeant) Charlie Harper took a group of the new ST volunteers out to the range for some instruction on the use of the LAW and claymore mines.

Each of the new men rigged a Claymore under Charlie's watchful eye and then set it off on an imaginary advancing enemy (a few empty 55 gallon drums down range). Both the explosion and the effect down range were very impressive, indeed. The claymore would work quite well to break enemy contact and discourage further pursuit. Charlie also warned us that the indigenous personnel had learned how to steal the C4 explosive from the Claymore mine to use cooking their food. C4 burns with a hot, blue flame, something like Sterno. To prevent the pilfering, the Claymores were issued to those who would carry them just before the mission.

After completing the Claymore training, Charlie brought out a few boxes of LAWS. He went over their use in detail and then had each of us fire two of the weapons at a target downrange. The LAW was a single shot 66mm anti tank rocket launcher that replaced the Bazooka after the Korean War. The LAW was a weapon that I did not like firing. The back blast out of the light expandable tubing was strong enough to cut a man in half. The weapon was fired with the tube resting on the shoulder and the ear right next to the tube when the sights were used to choose the target. When the rocket was fired the noise from the blast caused severe pain in my ear. I took cigarette filters, tore the paper off, wadded up the fibrous filter material, and pushed it into my ears in an attempt to deaden the sound. The filters had little effect and the pain from each firing was intense.

On this particular day, we had several duds that failed to fire. MSG Harper had us pile these dud weapons down range about 100 yards from our position and had one of the new guys, Sgt Mike Tucker get in the prone position and aim and fire a LAW at the pile. Mike scored a direct hit and the pile exploded with a huge cloud of fire and dust. Mike yelled that he was hit and I rushed over to check him out. Blood was spurting out of his neck near the carotid artery. I quickly stuck my finger in the hole and applied pressure to the bleeder. I looked up at MSG Harper and he appeared pale in his concern over his student. While holding pressure on the bleeder, I asked for one of the men to give me their tee shirt. I had him rip his shirt so I could fashion a makeshift pressure bandage. I applied the pressure dressing to Mike's neck and had him hold pressure over the bandage. We all loaded up in the deuce and a half and headed back to FOB 1 and the dispensary. Mike was treated and was in the Green Beret Lounge later in the day sharing stories over a cold beer.

Sgt Mike Tucker on the "range" with his CAR 15, Ron Zaiss photo

The experience had created respect between MSG Harper and us new guys, and he went above and beyond what was required in his training and friendship with us. Charlie was a quiet, humble man with a lot of recon experience. He had been on two previous tours in Vietnam and had been sent home both times after being critically injured while attempting to take NVA (North Vietnamese Army) prisoners. My understanding was that he had held some sort of US Army championship in Karate. Charlie never told us about his accomplishments in that regard, but put them to use in training us in hand to hand combat.

One day, as he covered how to disarm an enemy soldier in order to take him prisoner, he chose me as his guinea pig. After he went over the moves several times in slow motion he said that we were to perform it in quick time. The first time I was the enemy and I held an unloaded 45 pointed at him. Before I could pull the trigger, Charlie had me on the ground with the weapon out of my hand and a knife at my throat. I could not believe how quickly this forty something master sergeant had overpowered me. When I was back on my feet

Charlie had me practice the moves on him several times in slow motion. He then had me do the technique in quick time (without the knife). My first attempt at normal speed went well, however in my twenty-two year-old enthusiasm I had hurt my instructor's shoulder.

The move included sidestepping the armed man and cupping the man's wrist that was holding the weapon, with the right hand to prevent him from pointing the weapon at you. Next, the left hand would slide up to the enemy's shoulder. The wrist holding the weapon would be gripped and held out straight while pressure was applied to the man's shoulder. If enough pressure was applied, the shoulder would be dislocated. I had applied a little too much pressure to this older warriors shoulder and caused him unnecessary pain. Fortunately, this powerful man forgave me and the training continued.

One of the most important skills taught at Special Forces school at Fort Bragg, North Carolina was map reading and the use of the lensatic compass. The stateside training included nighttime compass courses through the North Carolina woods and swamps. The lesson learned was that if you did not do it perfectly, you would not get home for dinner or even the weekend. The training and practice of this skill continued in Vietnam. The One Zero (American team leader) would map out a compass course requiring map reading and compass skills and then have the team maneuver through the course for practice. All American team members would take their turns with the compass and topographical map to polish their skills. On a mission, all three American team members carried a compass and a topographical map of the target area. These items were carried on the person and not in the rucksack or on the web gear. If an American team member was separated from the team during the mission he had both the equipment and skill to call in airstrikes on the enemy or to call in for an extraction.

To understand the importance of this skill to the SOG teams, consider being dropped off in a hostile area behind enemy lines, in a thick triple canopy jungle where the US Government would deny your very existence. Now consider being all alone and trying to determine how you would find your way to an area where a friendly aircraft could pick you up. Furthermore, consider coming across an enemy element such as an antiaircraft gun with a number of enemy soldiers watching for the helicopter that can bring you back to safety. You can call in an airstrike, however, the only available aircraft is a B52 Stratofortress, which is carrying 4,000 pound bombs and is flying at 38,000 ft. Even though the enemy is 1,000 yards from you, these bombs are going to shake you like a mighty earthquake. You cannot see the plane nor can the bomber crew see you. You must quickly compare the terrain features against the map and pinpoint both your location and the enemy's location. Finally, you must instruct the navigator on both your location and that of the enemy, as well as the direction that you want him to fly over the target. Within a few minutes you will hear the single word "Dropped" and you know that it is time to get as low as possible. When the bombs impact the target, your body is actually lifted off the ground by the force of the explosions. Shrapnel, splintered trees and huge clumps of earth and rocks are thrown in the air by the force of the blast. If the bombs impact any closer than 1000 yards from your position you may not survive the explosion…or the flying debris. If your map reading was perfect, the enemy has been destroyed and you can be extracted from the newly created clearings in the dense jungle. Think about this next time you navigate using a street map in an unfamiliar city.

SFC Glenn Lane was my One Zero while I was assigned to ST Idaho. Glenn had a great sense of humor and enjoyed camaraderie with the team. He was creative in training the team and had a unique way of rewarding accurate compass and map work. On one practice mission, the team patrolled the rice paddies and jungle areas around the camp and ended up in the village of Phu Luong. Through the rice paddies, he had us on the dikes and we practiced hand signals, team movements, and firing positions as well as following the compass course that he had plotted for us. The day was very hot and humid, and by early afternoon we had entered the village of Phu Luong. We stopped a few times along the way and conversed with the friendly villagers through our interpreter Hiep. I also gave a few APC (Aspirin, Phenacitin and Caffeine) tablets to an old woman complaining about a headache, and cleaned and bandaged an injured foot on a young boy. These times were special for us all as villagers and the team would gather around to watch the American "Bac Si" (doctor) do his thing. The simple care and kindness went a long way to win the hearts and minds of the Vietnamese people. It was in sharp contrast to the VC of NVA who would go into a village, take the food and supplies of the villagers, and perhaps kill anyone who did not cooperate with them.

Ba Si De

The completion of the compass course was at a local gathering place in the village. It was a shack with some bench tables and seats covered by a corrugated tin roof, open on three sides.

The proprietor, "Papa San", invited us to have seats. Hiep asked if we wanted some soup and we all ordered a bowl. Mr. Tu, the teams Zero One (Vietnamese team leader) ordered "can wine" for the group. This rice wine (about 39% alcohol) was served in a large container with a long bamboo straw for each man. The small, colorful peppers in the noodle soup were hotter than hell and the turpentine taste of the rice wine did little to cool our burning mouths. In Vietnamese culture, it was considered very bad manners to stop drinking before the host and so we continued sipping through the straws until the container was empty. The indigenous personnel got a big kick out of the Americans suffering through the blistering soup and rice wine.

Our point man, Ha, challenged me to try a real mans drink. Rather than show weakness in front of my teammates, I accepted his challenge. He ordered up some Ba Si De for his friend. It was served to me in an aluminum canteen cup. The drink was only about two or three ounces in the bottom of the cup, but was a lethal spirit distilled from fermented rice. It was about 160 proof and similar to the moonshine I encountered during training in the Smokey Mountains of North Carolina. I offered to share it with Lane and the others, but was told that this one was for me alone. I drank it down and quickly forgot how hot the soup had been as we staggered back up Route One to the camp. This was one compass course that I would never forget.

The Ambush

My first combat mission was actually a "practice mission" with Spike Team Idaho and another Spike Team, plus a few other new guys. I do not remember all of the participants, but clearly remember Glenn Lane and Tim Kirk from ST Idaho, SFC Skau and fellow medic Ron Romancik. Both Spike Teams were fully manned with three Americans and nine Vietnamese soldiers. There were also a few extra men brought along to try by fire, so to speak. I remember one young black PFC (Private First Class) who had been assigned to Special Forces from some airborne unit. He was not actually a trained Special Forces soldier, but was brought along on this "training" mission to see where he might fit in to one of our combat units.

MACV (Military Assistance Command Vietnam) intelligence had recently learned that arms were being smuggled down the Perfume River into the city of Hue by sampans'. The smuggling was done under cover of darkness and the boats were moved along the river by NVA soldiers with poles. The operation was silent and passed through an area deemed pacified by the US Marines who "controlled" the area.

The training mission was run just like a regular SOG mission. The Americans went into the S2 (security) office and were briefed on the mission by the S2 officer. We were shown a large map of the target area and our ambush site was pointed out. We were told that the mission was for real and that it was chosen for training because of its close proximity to ground units to back us up as well as being within range of Marine and Naval artillery, should they be needed. After the briefing, the teams were assembled and each mans gear was checked by the senior NCOs on the mission. The men were then loaded in two trucks and driven off into the sunset.

The setting was perfect for a training mission or a movie set. The thirty or so men from SOG rode to a position close to the river in Deuce and a Half's in the waning light of the day. We unloaded from the trucks and lined up in a column with ST Idaho in the lead, a few new men in the middle, SFC Skau, and the second ST following. The group moved out in silence on a narrow trail, which had been previously been scouted by Skau

The vegetation was thick and lush as we approached the river bank. As the river came into view we could see that there was a natural, earthen berm about three feet high all along the shore. Skau was in charge and he directed that the column spread out at double arms length (about five feet between each man) along the bank. I was set up with ST Idaho to my right with Romancik, the new guys, Skau, and then the second Spike Team to my left. The ambush was set up with the team on the outside curve of a sharp bend in the river. Before complete darkness set in, we could see across the river which was about 100 yards wide at this location as well as a short distance both up and down the river. The teams were instructed to eat and then to stay awake and watch the river. Instruction was given that SFC Skau would give the order to fire at the appropriate time. We sat there staring into the darkness for what seemed like an eternity. The only sounds were the disease carrying mosquitoes buzzing around looking for a meal and an occasional fish breaking the surface of the water dining on a mosquito or other insect. The situation really made me think about the hunt and hunted universe that we were a part of this night.

The hours passed very slowly as every man vigilantly watched the darkness. We all strained our eyes trying to see something but the night was overcast and pitch black. Skau had carried a newly developed Starlight scope (night vision scope) that would let him see any movement on the river. The Marines had set a strict curfew on any river traffic at 9PM and anything on the river after that hour was fair game to our guns.

At about two in the morning, Skau launched a parachute flare over the river, jumped to his feet with an M60 machine gun on his hip and shouted, "Open fire!" The flare lit the river and the two sampans (flat bottomed river boat) traveling downstream about 75 yards ahead of us. Almost simultaneously with Skau's machine gun, we all opened fire with our CAR15s. The picture that I remember from that night beyond the Rambo like figure of Skau and his machine gun firing away was one of the hundreds of tracers from all of our weapons traveling across the water and converging on the Sampans. The VC or NVA aboard those boats did not stand a chance of survival (I don't even remember them returning fire). The boats exploded from the ordinance and ammunition they carried and burned before sinking in the river.

As the last flickers of light from the sinking sampans shimmered across the water, Skau called for a cease fire. Silence and darkness once again blanketed the scene. Suddenly, the stillness was shattered by the hysterical voice of the PFC whom I mentioned earlier. He was shouting that he was seeing "little people shooting silver rockets out of cardboard tubes." Skau moved to his position and ordered him to be still. The PFC continued in his hysteria and eventually Skau slapped him one across the face which quieted him down. Skau was talking quietly trying to calm him down and assure him that we were safe.

We don't know for sure what happened to the young PFC that night, but surmised that he suffered from the classic shell shock described in the second World War or that he had hallucinated from the dexamyl that he had taken to stay alert for the ambush. At any rate, he was deemed unfit to serve with SOG and was shipped back to his unit the following day. Nothing more happened during the long, sleepless night and at first light, Skau radioed for the trucks and cautiously lead the team back to the pre arranged rendezvous.

Since this was the first official combat mission for Romancik and I, SFC Skau came around to our hooch (living place or shelter) the following day and informed Ron Romancik and I that we qualified for either the Combat Infantry Man badge (CIB) or the Combat Medical Badge (CMB). Being proud to have been selected for and having successfully trained and qualified as Special Forces Medics, Ron and I both Choose the CMB.

The Ambulance parked in front of the "new" dispensary.

I would spend the remainder of my tour serving as an ST member, only working as a medic between missions or when someone was wounded in combat. Ron would spend his tour doing what we had been trained for. He worked in the dispensary, flew as chase medic during insertions and extractions, and handled medical assignments such as the "rat patrol." Ron even performed a one man "Bright Light Mission" where he rescued an American from behind enemy lines the day after he had been injured and isolated in a Marine helicopter crash. He was a good medic and a good friend.

Bac Si

The Combat Medical Badge (CMB) depicts a military type stretcher overlaid with the medical symbol of the winged cross denoting swift care. Under the cross is a staff with intertwined serpents. The medical symbol was developed long ago from the story of Moses and the Israelites recorded in the Pentateuch book of Numbers, Chapter 21:

> *Verse 6. And the Lord sent fiery serpents among the people, and they bit the people; and much people of Israel died. 7. Therefore the people came to Moses, and said, We have sinned, for we have spoken against the Lord, and against thee; pray unto the Lord, that he take away the serpents from us. And Moses prayed for the people. 8. And the Lord said unto Moses, make thee a fiery serpent, and set it upon a pole: and it shall come to pass, that every one that is bitten, when he looketh upon it, shall live. 9. And Moses made a serpent of brass, and put it upon a pole, and it came to pass, that if a serpent had bitten any man, when he beheld the serpent of brass, he lived."* (Numbers 21:6-9)

The Green Berets of FOB 1 were like an extended family and each of us had our "chores" to do. The Commanding Officer would assign one of the men who were not assigned to an ST or Hatchet Force to perform any major renovation or improvement in the camp and then many of us would pitch in to help.

Special Forces medics are highly trained and capable of handling many situations normally reserved for doctors. Their skills ranged from performing surgeries to the diagnosis and treatment of diseases almost unheard of back in the United States. The indigenous population of the camp, and sometimes the sick from the village of Phu Luong, would come seeking treatment for a wide variety of maladies. The Vietnamese people were loving and kind and really appreciated the care they received at the hands of these American "doctors."

Since I was trained as a Special Forces Medic (MOS 91B4S), I worked in the dispensary on most of my days not spent in training or on combat missions. It was here that we held sick call each day for our fifty Americans and the five-hundred or so indigenous personnel who lived or worked in the camp. Our team of medics diagnosed and treated everything from the common cold to Falciparum Malaria. We had a fully-equipped laboratory where we could do routine blood and urine testing as well as more elaborate testing for tropical parasites. We also had a functional operating room where we would do wound debridement's or whatever else might be necessary in an emergency. In addition we would do dental work when it became necessary including temporary fillings and extractions.

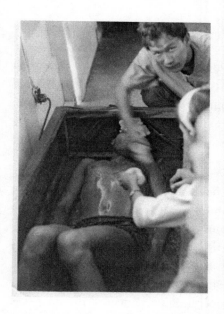

An indigenous malaria patient is being treated to an ice bath to reduce his critically high body temperature of 106. Note the "bathtub" is a simple wooden box lined with military issue ponchos. The caretakers are several of the Vietnamese medical staff who worked in the FOB1 dispensary

On a normal morning at FOB 1, one or more of the camp's medics would be off flying chase for a team insertion or extraction while the others would be staffing the dispensary. Outside the door of the dispensary, a line would form with anywhere from ten to fifty men and women seeking medical help. The dispensary also employed several indigenous personnel as nurses and interpreters. As the patients got to the door, they were questioned about their ailment or injury and then sent to one of the examination rooms to be seen by a Green Beret "Bac Si" (Vietnamese for doctor). It was here in the examining rooms where wounds were cleaned and dressed, where blood was drawn, and where difficult diagnoses were made and treated.

One day I visited the local hospital in Hue with some of my fellow medics and was horrified by what I saw. It was the Hue Central Hospital, which was first established in 1894. Its location was directly across the Perfume River from the Royal Palace. As we walked into what we expected to be the lobby, we encountered a surrealistic scene of a makeshift operating room. To the side of the temporary operating table and lights was a table. It was piled high with mangled arms and legs amputated from the injured or infected and sprinkled with some sort of white powder, apparently sprinkled here to reduce the stench and discourage the horde of flies hovering above. The blood splattered walls, the old marble floors and the powdered body parts were the perfect setting for an Alfred Hitchcock film. It seemed that the hospital in the old capital was out of supplies and loaded with the injured of the Tet offensive. We shared from our stores of morphine, antibiotics and antiseptics; and we took home a new understanding of the need for treating the indigenous in our care.

In Vietnam, a simple cut on the foot could have cost a man a leg… or even his life. Tetanus and gangrene were common; and both could usually be prevented with simple care. And so, wounds were cleaned and bandaged, tetanus shots and antibiotics were administered, and patients were told to return so the dressings could be changed and the wounds re-examined. If a wound required sutures, it was normally left open for three days (to check for infection) and then stitched up. Standard operating procedure at the time was to treat all injured patients with penicillin and streptomycin to prevent infection.

I remember feeling very proud one day when an American Lieutenant came to the dispensary with an AK-47 bullet wound to his leg. I offered to send him up the road three miles to the Marine field hospital to be treated by a Marine doctor. He said that he did not trust those Marine physicians and would rather have one of his own medics perform the necessary surgery. Since the wound was through the fleshy part of the calf and involved no bone, nerve, or major blood vessel, I suited up and scrubbed to perform his surgery while one of the Vietnamese staff cleaned him up, readying him for the procedure. I gave the Lieutenant injectable lidocane to block the pain, cleaned the wound, debreided some damaged tissue, and bandaged him up instructing him to return the following day for dressing change. It was a simple procedure. The wound healed nicely and was closed on the fourth day without any infection or other complication. From that day forward, I was referred to as "Doc Perry" by the Lieutenant and his teammates. Many others in the camp called me "Doc" but I had earned this man's respect the hard way.

I also enjoyed the diagnostic work in the lab and spent considerable time there backing up the other medics who were seeing the patients, taking samples, and administering medications.

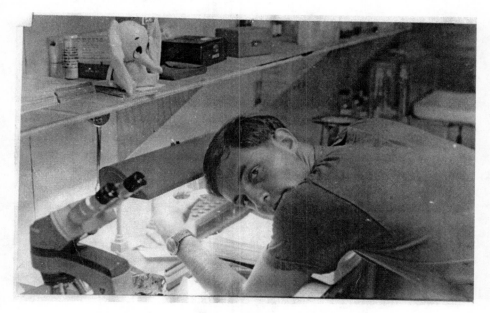

Steve Perry working in the new lab, March 1968

When I first arrived at FOB 1, the dispensary was really too small to handle all the medical needs of the camp. We were given one of the vacant buildings, built up on stilts, to set up as we liked for the new dispensary. Since I had a secondary MOS of combat engineer and had some back home experience in construction, I volunteered to direct the indigenous carpenters in remodeling the rustic building into a usable dispensary. The local carpenters had no power tools and made all cuts using a rustic sort of bow saw. They proved themselves to be very proficient with their tools and did a great job on the new dispensary. They helped us frame partitions for a waiting room, three examination rooms, a pharmacy, an operating room and a lab. I scrounged up lab equipment and supplies from a Marine corpsman stationed nearby. I also traded an AK47 for a forklift operator at Da Nang airbase to load a few pallets of air conditioners, surgical lamps and an autoclave aboard a Blackbird headed to Phu Bai. I don't know where the supplies were headed, but we really needed them at FOB 1.

In the lab and pharmacy, I instructed the carpenters to build cabinets and shelves to house the diagnostic equipment and medications. Even a sink was installed in the lab; however, we had no running water, so a refillable five gallon water bottle with a spout and surgical tubing served as a source of water. Another length of tubing was attached to the sinks drain, allowing the sink to drain under the dispensary on the sandy soil. It was in this lab that the mystery of many illnesses was uncovered. Microscopic parasites in the blood, abnormal blood counts, and other findings were extremely important to diagnosis and treatment of tropical diseases.

The new building was large enough to facilitate living quarters for all of the medics assigned to FOB 1; and it was decided that it would be wise to quarter all the medics together so that they were readily available to go to work in a medical emergency. Sometime after my roommate Ken was killed in early May, I moved into the new barracks with my brother medics. The quarters were filled with stacked bunk beds and footlockers. Reel to reel tape recorders from AKAI, TEAC, and SONY blasted out the sounds of Jimi Hendrix, The Rolling Stones, and Peter Paul and Mary. The best part of the new housing was the air conditioners that I had rescued from the airfield in Da Nang. That pallet of air conditioners cooled the entire dispensary and our housing area to a comfortable, dry 70 degrees around the clock. Our housing quickly became the "cool place" to hang out and listen to the sounds of the 60s or share cookies and brownies from the "care packages" we received from home.

The medics I remembered here were Bruce Johnston, Ron Romancik, James Vernon, Jerry Donely, and Terry Oberhardt. I am sure there were other medics who passed through on TDY (temporary duty), from the 1st Special Group in Okinawa, or who served on STs or Hatchet Forces in the camp.

We would sit around during the quiet times and share stories of home or talk about the most recent unusual diagnosis or adventure of a medic flying chase.

After returning from the hospital the second time I was wounded, I spent most of my time working around the dispensary or doing other duties around the camp. Admittedly, my medical experiences in Vietnam were far more limited than my brother medics due to my assignment to the STs for the majority of my tour.

SOG Medic Bruce Johnston 1968

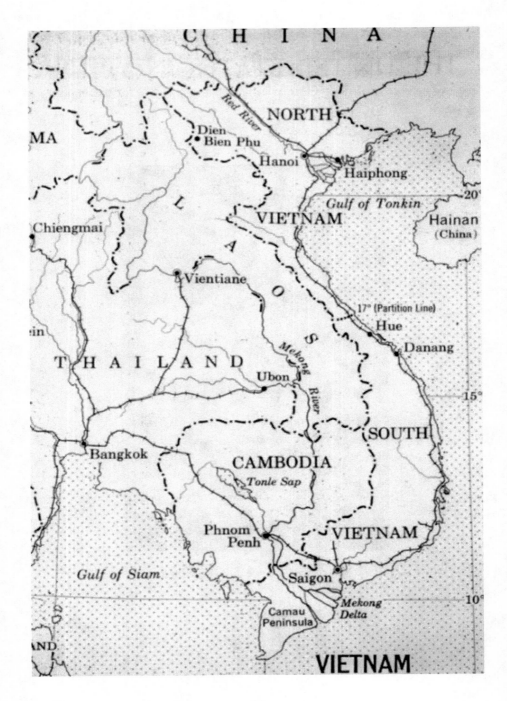

Valley of Death

ST Idaho was called to stand formation before the team house to be inspected by the teams One Zero, SFC Glenn Lane. Lane was a weathered, lanky, six-foot two inch Texan with a long history of service with the US Special Forces. We had heard tales that he had been on a team in South America that had hunted down and killed the legendary Che'. Like our missions behind enemy lines, the US has officially denied any part in Che's death. Today, Lane was our Spike Team (ST) leader and was inspecting the team's full complement of nine indigenous mercenaries and three Americans. I was the teams second in command or One One and Tim Kirk was the One Two or radio operator. Others I remember that day were Hiep Nguyen, the team's interpreter, Ha, the fearless and stealthy point man, and Mister Tu, the older and more experienced Zero-One (indigenous team leader).

To describe ST Idaho as a scary group of men would be an understatement. The men stood in full battle dress complete with camouflaged paint on the exposed flesh of their faces and necks, blackened uniforms void of any labels or identifying marks, web gear, side arms, rucksacks and weapons. On this particular day, ten men carried Colt CAR15s. These are fully automatic 5.56mm assault rifles with identifying information such as serial numbers machined off so that the weapons could not be traced back to the US if the team was killed or captured. The weapons were carried on braided green rope slings, carefully sized so that the weapon could be carried at exactly at the right position at ones hip to be fired instantly when needed without having to shoulder the weapon. The team had spent many hours at the range practicing this firing technique until each of the team members could regularly hit an enemy target with two to three rounds in a diagonal pattern across the chest at 40-50 feet. The remaining two team members carried M79 grenade launchers and an assortment of 40mm rounds for their weapons. The weapon was usually carried loaded with a canister round. This was the equivalent of a

40mm shot gun round with large 00 pellets. This load allowed the grenadier to quickly fire on an enemy in the dense jungle, which was our area of operation.

In preparation for this day, Lane, Kirk and I had attended a briefing at S2 the previous day, where we were advised that Spike Team Idaho was to be inserted in target Tango 4, deep inside the Ashau Valley (the "Valley of Death"). For security reasons, the team was told to ready itself for a five day mission; however, no specific target information was given to the indigenous personnel. S2 informed us that there had been a major increase in reported enemy traffic and buildup along the Ho Chi Min trail near Tango 4.

After the briefings, Lane and I were driven by Jeep to the airstrip at the 1st Marine Division Base, located three kilometers south of FOB 1. There, we boarded an Air Force 02 Covey plane to fly over our target area for VR (visual recon) and to pick a LZ (landing zone). The O2 "Skymaster" was a propeller driven, four passenger plane made by Cessna and flown by an Air Force Major. The plane had propellers in front of and behind the cockpit and a split tail; and it was used for VR and FAC (forward air controller) work. The weather was clear with temperatures in the nineties, but the humidity was unbearable. It was a relief to finally take off and get out of the steam bath-like climate.

We watched in awe as the Skymaster rose above the Marine Base, the huge ammo dump, the range where we trained the team, the rice paddies, and the village of Phu Luong. Quickly, all signs of civilization faded and there were only rolling hills covered by the dense vegetation of the jungle. The target area was about 50 miles from the airbase; and as the hills disappeared behind us, the steep mountains and valleys of the border region appeared. The cool air inside the plane was refreshing and provided some sense of comfort on this day aloft.

Small clearings appeared scattered in the lush vegetation of the mountainsides. Some of the clearings were slash and burn clearings where the Montagnard people lived and raised their crops. Others were bomb craters from earlier airstrikes. Each disturbed the seemingly endless and tranquil jungle canopy as we "floated" about two-thousand-feet above in our air-conditioned cabin. Stillness and beauty were slashed by the eruption of anti-aircraft gunfire and by tracers cutting through the air around us. There was little that we could do, but sit and hope that none of the bullets or explosions of anti-aircraft rounds found its' mark. The O2 pilot, on the other hand, took evasive action by diving down to about 500 feet above the treetops. The pilot also called in the coordinates of the anti- aircraft guns to the Navy ships offshore. Their 16-inch guns could deliver high explosive rounds on the target with pinpoint accuracy. We, on the other hand, continued on our flight to the northwest to complete our VR, which was our mission of the day. As we flew along at this low altitude, we observed brief openings in the canopy revealing dirt roads. At one point, we spotted enemy vehicles and scattered troops on the ground. Some began firing their rifles at us and the pilot climbed again to a more comfortable altitude, out of reach of the would-be assassins.

As we rose in altitude, we got our first glimpse of the Ashau Valley. It lay ahead of us along a broad ridge line. The valley floor was almost devoid of vegetation and pocked with thousands of large bomb craters where B-52s unloaded their ordinance night after night in attempts to slow the advance of North Vietnams troops and their supplies to the south. It was here that many brave men on both sides had given their lives in this war, and were I would lose many good friends, and leave a piece of myself forevermore.

As we banked toward the north, our pilot advised us that we had just crossed the border into Laos. After a few more miles, he told us that we had reached the Tango 4 target area. Lane and I scanned the steep terrain just across the ridge-line and eventually spotted what appeared to be an old clearing which was overgrown with elephant grass and other shrubs and vines. From our altitude, the area looked open enough and suitable for our insertion helicopter to hover as the team members rappelled down ropes to the ground. We did one more fly over of the area and carefully marked the LZ position on our military topo (topographic) maps. No other suitable LZs were seen in the AO(Area of Operation). Our pilot climbed to a higher altitude and headed back toward Phu Bai.

As we flew along the ridge line, the pilot pointed out the old airstrip and the remains of the Ashau Special Forces camp, which had been overrun two years before. The view of the valley and its violent past reminded me of the 23rd Psalm. *"Yea, though I walk through the valley of the shadow of death, I will fear no evil."* I could not recall the rest as written in scripture, and rejected the local inscriptions I had seen engraved on lighters and displayed boldly on a plaque in the Gunfighter Saloon. Those quotes finished the verse, "because I am the meanest M-Fer in the valley..." and even though I had not practiced my faith in many years, I had no intentions of blaspheming God while engaged in a deadly war. One day in May of 1968, the verse and its' meaning became very clear to me as I was lying, seriously injured and surrounded by a large enemy element in that same "Valley of Death."

When we returned to FOB 1, it was "chow" time; and our team members had gathered their meals and were eating in the Team Room. Lane and I grabbed a few cold beers and joined our Vietnamese friends. Lane informed the team that we would launch on a mission at 1100hrs in the morning and instructed everyone to pack up, load magazines and clean their weapons. We were all directed to stand ready for an inspection of our gear at 1030hrs and be ready to launch at that time. The team members had been training hard for the past two weeks and were happy to be going out to "kill some VC."

Launch day arrived and the team assembled for inspection. SFC Glenn Lane inspected each mans' weapon, side arm, ammunition and other ordinance he required each man to carry. Additional ordinance consisted of Claymore mines (for perimeter defense), M-14 (toe popper) mines, hand-grenades, smoke-grenades (to mark targets), pen flares, assorted radios and listening devices, booby-trapped enemy ammunition ("Eldest Son"), and sometimes light anti-tank weapons (LAWs) to stop enemy convoys. Laws were also useful in breaking enemy contact if the team was being chased. Every man also carried his own canteens of water and a small food ration for eating over the planned five-day mission.

The Radio man carried a heavy PRC25 radio, which he could use to talk to friendly planes in the air above the team, as well as remote military and CIA radio sites. Each of the Americans carried a small squad radio taped to their web gear for internal communications between the team members, as well as an emergency radio, called the URC 10. This was a foolproof little radio that was two pieces connected by a heavy black cable. The radio was carried in the two breast pockets of the jungle fatigue with the wire running behind the neck. In an emergency, the microphone (mike) was keyed and locked on. This little radio broadcast a constant homing signal on a frequency monitored by all friendly aircraft. If an aircraft picked up the signal, attempted contact, and the American on the ground did not key the mike to respond with appropriate code words and identifiers, the radio was assumed to be in enemy hands and the radios' position would be promptly bombed. If an American answered the aircraft, rescue operations could be arranged or airstrikes could be called in on targets of opportunity. The URC 10 helped save the lives of surviving team members when a team was split up or lost during combat operations.

Every team member carried a few battle dressings but as a trained Special Forces medic, I also carried a supply of morphine surettes, a pair of hemostats a few life saving medications,and a supply of Dexamyl. This drug is a mixture of dextroamphetamine and amobarbitals and was used to keep the entire team awake and alert through the night when we were in a particularly dangerous position behind enemy lines. Stateside, the drug became famous in 1966 when the Rolling Stones released the song "Mothers Little Helper", which told of how a variation of the pill helped mother get through her busy day.

I do not know the actual weight of all the equipment, weapons, ammunition, and explosives carried by each SOG team member, but my estimate would be between 75 and 100 pounds. To make matters worse, one must consider the steep terrain, the dense jungle, and intense heat and humidity ever present in the AO. When a hostile force was encountered, the team was forced to break contact by its initial burst of firepower. When the enemy force was not killed or repelled, the team relied on the skill of the One Zero to lead the team in escape and evasion (E&E) which many times involved running through the jungle carrying the weight of all that equipment. Today, 40 years later, I cannot fathom how we were able to carry such a load through the hostile and steamy jungles of the Ashau. Our enemy was in his own backyard, light afoot with only an AK47, a light ammo belt, and a few grenades, yet our Spike Teams were usually able to break contact and lose themselves once again in the jungle.

As the inspection was nearly complete, three Sikorski H34 helicopters (code name "Kingbee") flew low overhead, circled the camp, and landed on the airstrip just across the road, while three Marine Huey Gunships circled overhead. Lane walked the team past the team rooms, the S2 office, and the officer's barracks out the front gate to the waiting choppers across the road. Lane and I checked each of the choppers to ensure that the OD (olive drab) nylon rappelling ropes were securely fastened with bowlines. The 120 foot ropes had to support team members and their equipment as they rappelled into the LZ. Lane instructed the team to mount up with Tim, Hiep, Ha, Lane and two other indigenous in the first chopper, while the remaining team members and I were in the second chopper. The third Kingbee carried one of the SOG medics from Phu Bai and was referred to as the "chase chopper." If one of the insertion choppers went down, the chase chopper was to swoop down, pick up the survivors, and the medic was there to treat the wounded on the flight back to the FOB. He carried a medical kit with lifesaving IVs medicines and battle dressings. After forty-years, I cannot remember the name of the medic on this particular mission, but it must have been one of my close friends: Ron Romancik, Jerry Donley, or Bruce Johnston.

The Kingbees had the doors removed and were manned by Vietnamese pilots and a crew chief/door gunner. A 30 caliber air-cooled machine gun was mounted on the Starboard (right side) side of each chopper. As I looked out of the chopper toward the road, I noticed an open Jeep with conventional uniformed U.S. soldiers peering at our "armed to the teeth" band of camouflage painted unconventional warriors mounted up in unconventional, unmarked, black and green helicopters. It is no wonder that the local conventional forces referred to us as "spooks", "sneaky Pete" or "snake eaters." We did look the part and were a truly scary lot.

As the Marine gunships passed overhead, the Kingbees revved up and lifted off in a great cloud of dust. We rose to an altitude of about 500-ft, and were relieved of the heat and humidity by the rush of air past the open sides of the chopper, as we headed northwest toward the "Valley of Death." As I sat in the open door, watching the dense jungle roll by under my feet, I was impressed with the beauty and the diversity of the jungle. I thought back to a classroom at Orange Coast College in Costa Mesa where I studied Botany and the diversity of the rainforest. I thought of my family and of how they would enjoy this flight over the green carpet of Southeast Asia. These peaceful thoughts quickly vanished as tracers sliced by my open door.

The door gunner yelled, "VC", as he opened fire with his machine gun into the clearing along a roadside below. The mayhem soon ended and the serenity of the flight and the jungle carpet returned. I can honestly say that the only two times I was afraid in Vietnam was while in a chopper being fired on from the ground, and when I was near death on a Bright Light mission in target Whiskey-Five a few months later. I don't know if it was my life experiences, the intense training and confidence in my war brothers or the foolishness of youth, but I felt invincible and almost bullet-proof on most missions. It would not be long before the reality of war would sweep such thoughts from my mind. For today, I was ready to enter this foreign jungle and fight beside my team members because I trusted them with my life… and "I feared no evil."

Our helicopters flew in sort of a loose formation with Lane's chopper leading to the LZ, mine second, and the chase chopper behind. Slightly above and behind chase were the three Marine gunships loaded with rocket-launchers and miniguns. As we approached the LZ, the gunships swooped down and made a low pass to detect any enemy presence or draw fire from the ground. As the gunships climbed and circled above, the lead Kingbee moved over the LZ to a height of about 80-90 feet above the vegetation, and the six team members quickly rappelled down the 120 ft ropes to the ground. As their Kingbee pulled away, ours moved into position and we rappelled down. Our chopper was a little too high; and I went right off the end of the rope and nearly landed atop Lane. The landing was hard and racked my body with pain.

Although we wore gloves to protect our hands, my palms and fingers were blistered from the fast trip down the rope. Wasting no time, the Kingbee flew away and the gunships made another low pass over our position.

The team gathered and Ha lead us up the very steep hill through tangled brush, vines and elephant grass. As we approached the edge of the clearing, Lane motioned to Ha in well-practiced hand signs to scout ahead. The LZ was much steeper than it had appeared to us from 2,000-feet above the day before; and the tangle and thorns of the "wait a minute" vines slowed our movement significantly. The vines had long, thin branches with the strange botanical adaptation of the thorns pointing down the stems toward the roots of the plant. This configuration was perfect for hooking and holding clothing or skin, thus the name "Wait a Minute Vines." I made a mental note to take great care in choosing an LZ if I were ever called upon to do so. The thorns ripped at our clothing and flesh as the sun baked our overheated bodies. It was a real relief to see Ha at the tree-line motioning the team to advance into the shade and shelter of the jungle. As we entered the tree line, Lane had Tim call in a "team clear" to the still circling gunships, thus signaling them to return to their base.

As the sound or the rotors faded into the distance, the reality of our small team's position and vulnerability became evident. Here we were, twelve men alone on a mountainside, about 50-miles from all friendly forces, out of the protective reach of friendly artillery, and a long helicopter flight for any rescue if it became necessary. To make matters worse, we were behind enemy lines in Laos, a country that *our* country denied we ever entered until thirty-five years later. We had nothing to identify us as American citizens or soldiers. Only a handful or "spooks" knew where we were and what we were doing in the Ashau Valley. Those "in the know" were in the White House, the Pentagon, MACV SOG headquarters and back in Phu Bai. B-52 pilots flying bombing missions (sorties) over the Ashau knew that something was happening in our six-quare-kilometer target area; and that they were not to drop bombs on the target area or the one- kilometer buffer around it. It was comforting to know that the B-52s were up there somewhere, but they were so high up that they could not normally be seen or heard. Whether or not they existed was a matter of faith…until the day they were called upon to unload their deadly cargo on an enemy target.

The Jungle in this target area looked very different on the ground than it had from O-2. There were three distinct layers of old growth trees above our heads (referred to as a triple-canopy jungle). The tallest were massive hardwoods such as teak and mahogany, some four or five-feet in diameter at the base and 100-feet or so tall. Under them was another layer, fanning out with the branches and leaves covering an area perhaps 50 to 75 feet above the ground, and then the lowest layer at 20 to 40 ft. I was awestruck by the beauty of this place. Below the canopies existed an ecosystem as diverse as any I have ever experienced. The flora was made up of all the tropical plants, treasured in the US for tropical gardens and potted plants. There were stands of bamboos, hanging vines, and many colorful bromeliads and orchids. Interesting sizes, shapes, and colors of fungi thrived here, moistened by the almost constant dripping of water droplets from the canopy above. A pungent odor like rotting organic material and damp soil filled this place, which I have only experienced in a few other places on earth. Each encounter with this musky odor in later years has immediately transported me mentally to that day, time, and place.

As we continued towards the ridgeline, a few rifle shots cracked in the jungle a distance beyond our LZ. Lane told us in a whisper that it was probably NVA trackers trying to pick up our location by drawing our return fire. This, he referred to as recon-by-fire. He told the tail gunner and I to cover any trail we were leaving and to plant a few toe poppers to give us early warning if we were followed. We each armed and planted three of the small, plastic mines along our back trail and carefully marked their position on my map. This information would be transferred to S2 and MACV at our debriefing in hopes that some future mission would not cross this area unaware of the mines we left behind.

As we finally crossed over the ridgeline, Ha motioned for all to stop, be silent and on guard. Soon, Lane motioned me forward to observe a broad trail, with the jungle soil hard packed by many feet. The trail was so well used that there was little leaf litter on it and we discovered the remains of some light cardboard packaging on the trail. Perhaps the wrappings were the remains of some NVA soldier's lunch. The trail was marked on our maps and 35mm pictures were taken of it and the cardboard debris along it. There was a sharp bend in the trail just ahead; and Lane decided to have the team first cross the trail and then set up an ambush to attempt a prisoner snatch. The team was carefully spread out along the trail in hidden firing positions behind trees and berms. Claymore mines were set facing in both directions, both up and down the trail, and the team laid silently for more than an hour waiting for "Charlie" to appear. The snatching of a prisoner was dangerous business, indeed, and would offer both great risk and reward to the team. Colonel Warren, SOG Commander in Da Nang, had promised a little RR (rest and relaxation) trip to a remote island off the coast for any team who brought home a live prisoner. Their value was in the intelligence information which could be gleaned from them. The obvious risk was grabbing an armed enemy soldier in his own territory, surrounded by his comrades, in an area so far removed from any assistance or chance of rescue.

This time, the ambush produced nothing more than a brief rest from the torturous climb, giving time to think and listen to the jungle. We heard many sounds along the trail. An occasional bird or monkey, the constant drone of a circadid like insect, and then the high pitched sound of what we believed to be some sort of generator down in the valley. With the daylight getting short, Lane had us pack up the Claymores and start down the slope diagonally to the ridge line in search of a spot to spend the night or RON (remain over night). After walking for about another hour, we came across a piece of high ground that was flat and protected enough for the team to RON. Claymore mines were placed facing toward our back trail and also covering two other clear approaches to our position. Lane thought the RON position to be somewhat secure and put the team to bed with two men awake at all times, rotating their shifts every two hours.

The team settled down to dine on rice, raisins, and nuts. I had splurged and carried a c-ration can of sliced peaches, which really hit the spot this hot evening. SOG teams carried no tents, or any sleeping bags and each team member simply stretched out a nylon parka on which to sleep. I was on the first watch and leaned against a tree with weapon at the ready, listening to the night as darkness fell over the team. I noticed that the leaf and branch litter glowed in the dark and lit up the jungle floor with an eerie, blue-green light. I later learned that the glow was caused by a species of fungi that helped break down the thick layer of leaf litter. It thrived in the dense shade of the jungle and the ever-damp, humid conditions.

As I rested against that tree, I thought of camping with my friends long ago in the mountains and deserts of Southern California. We also had slept without tents or bags as we hiked the Silver Moccasin and Golden Arrowhead trails. I thought of the time that I had been tapped out for the Order of the Arrow by a young man dressed as an Indian brave. I was then taken silently out in the woods and left alone for the night, far removed from the other boy scouts. I had slept that night on the pine needles without fear and now I was in this place, alone with my thoughts and my sleeping war brothers. As I sat there silently, staring into the darkness, I heard distant voices and was reminded of the many dangers that existed here in the jungles of Laos. The voices reminded me of the men we were hunting and those who hunted us, but the danger here was also in the deadly snakes and spiders that lived in the jungle. There were plenty of mosquitoes that carried a number of deadly diseases and parasites such as Malaria, Leschmaniasis, and Dengue Fever. We protected ourselves, to some degree, with medications, as well as soaking our jungle fatigues in 90% DEET (N,N-Diethyl-meta-toluamide). This method worked so well that I never had a single mosquito bite during my tour of duty in Vietnam. We also coated the tops of our jungle boots and the bottom of our trousers with leach-repellent. The jungle floor crawled with land leeches, which were attracted to the CO_2 (carbon dioxide) that we exhale. I had heard stories of them crawling into body orifices with painful results.

My two hour "guard duty" ended without incident. I woke my replacement and laid down on my rain poncho for some rest. The voices I had heard earlier must have been NVA walking along that trail we had crossed earlier since the voices had faded into the distance. I slept most of the night with *peaceful* dreams of leeches, mosquitoes, and snakes. I awoke at first light to the sounds of movement. My team members were stirring and packing up for the day. Kirk was whispering into the mike of his PRC25. I heard from Lane later that he was talking to covey, reporting our encoded position, intended direction of travel, and the information of the trail and its night travelers. The other watches had also heard the voices passing in the night and they all seemed to be travelling toward South Vietnam in a South Easterly direction. After a few raisins and a gulp of water to wash down the daily dose of chloroquine primiquine (anti- malarial drug), the team packed up, took their positions and set off for another long hot day in the Valley.

The day dragged on as we silently and slowly moved through the jungle like a snake, twelve men weaving back and forth in line and stopping frequently to watch or listen. We travelled up and down the smaller ridges and valleys leading down into the Ashau. We crossed two trails along our way; and addressed the usual precautions of covering our tracks, planting mines in our back trail, and marking on our maps their locations. In the late afternoon we came across an open area where it appeared that many men; potentially NVA, had spent the night. The area had packed-down vegetation where they had slept, the remains of a few old campfire sites where they had cooked their rice, and other obvious signs of enemy habitation. Mr. Tu, our well seasoned tracker and survivor of the battle of Dien Bien Phu (1954), pointed out things that I would have overlooked and explained through our interpreter, Hiep, that this was an area where, perhaps, a company-sized group of NVA had spent the night recently. It was here that we carefully placed the small, cardboard box of enemy ammunition. In the box were twenty rounds of genuine AK47 ammunition in their original packing. One round had been intentionally altered by someone back in the US as a top secret war tactic to explode the breach of the enemy weapon when fired. This "altered" ammunition was code named "Eldest Son" and was intended not only to kill or maime, the enemy combatant, but to have a devastating psychological effect on the enemy troops, causing them to be wary of their own and captured weapons and ammunition. We took several photographs of the area and moved on lower into the Valley.

As the daylight began to fade we crossed a small stream of clear water. Lane ordered a short break so that the team could fill their canteens. I preferred to nurse the purified water in my canteens before I would drink this potentially parasite infested water. We could not risk a fire to boil the water, so it was better to ration the purified water I had carried from Phu Bai.

After crossing the stream, we climbed again up the slope of the small valley. After another 30 minutes or so, we came across a piece of high ground suitable for our RON. Claymores were placed defensively around our position and the team settled down for the night. Kirk tried to raise Covey to provide our position report and a team OK as we ate our evening meal. My meal consisted of rice and, raisins along with the big treat of the day, a pair of chocolate chip cookies, hand-made for me by my mother back in Huntington Beach, California. Perimeter guards were assigned and as the light faded into our second night, we saw the twinkling of campfires both above and below us in the distance. We could smell the fires and the faint smell of food cooking, but for us, dinner was meager and cold. The enemy was around us in all directions, but so far it seemed that our presence had been undetected.

I was awakened at 0100hrs by a ground-shaking explosion. When I awoke and readied my CAR 15 for a fight, I saw that my teammates were doing the same. Peering out into the darkness, we noticed what appeared to be men carrying lanterns and heading slowly in our direction. Meanwhile, Lane had determined that one of our Claymores had exploded spontaneously either from static electricity or radio waves from some unknown source. At any rate, the explosion had comprised our position; and Lane ordered the team to saddle up and to move up the steep slope of the ridge "at the double". As ordered, we all grabbed our gear and set off on a speedy trip up the ridgeline. We moved much more quickly that our normal pace and continued uphill through the darkness for about one hour. Our trek was slowed somewhat by the vengeful thorns of the "wait a minute vines," but eventually we arrived at another flat area with a thin canopy overhead. Lane told us to set up a perimeter and to rest here, but not to fall asleep. He then proceeded to plot our position and have Kirk attempt to quietly raise anyone on our emergency frequencies. Eventually, Tim made contact with someone and handed the mike over to the One Zero. In a coded message, Lane told the contact who we were, where we were, and requested the message be relayed to SOG and that our extraction be arranged at this location at first light. He also told the contact that there was no LZ, and that our extraction would require either a jungle penetrator or McGuire rigs. After closing communications, we waited in the still darkness for the first rays of light to appear.

None too soon, the first light of morning appeared through the 25' opening in the canopy above. Shortly thereafter, we heard the unmistakable sound of helicopters. Kirk contacted the rescue choppers, reconfirmed our latitude and longitude, and described the terrain and the broken canopy overhead. As the choppers got closer, we fired pen flares up through the opening until we were spotted; and the first chopper responded by dropping four McGuire Rigs down through the trees. The McGuire Rig was a 3 inch wide strap configured as a big loop at the end of a rappelling rope. The rig also had a small, self-tightening noose near the top, which tightened on the rider's wrist as a safety. The rider would stick his wrist through the noose and sit in the strap to be hauled up as the helicopter rose above. I would learn to respect this simple device as I rode it to safety on six later missions with SOG.

The choppers were not the old Kingbee that had inserted us two days earlier, but Hueys on loan with their crews from B229[th] Assault Helicopter Bn of the First Calvary. Our missions took top priority; and so when transportation was needed in a hurry, all we had to do was ask and MACV would provide. As Ordered by the One Zero, I got situated in one of the rigs with three of the Vietnamese; and the chopper rose, dragging me through the treetops. When we cleared the treetops, the pilot dropped right down into the barren valley floor and gently lowered us onto the long, abandoned airstrip. We hurriedly pulled up our ropes and rigs, and climbed into the helicopter just as it rose again above the bomb-cratered airstrip. As we rose and headed home, we could see the next chopper approaching with four of our teammates dangling in their McGuire rigs about 100 feet below. Farther up the hill from where we had just been extracted, we could see the third Slick lifting Lane, Kirk, and the others to safety. There were also a few gunships circling above... just in case.

The 45-minute flight back to FOB 1 was uneventful and so my first mission "across the fence" into Laos had been completed without a scratch, except for those inflicted by the "wait a minute vines." It was truly an experience that remains vivid in my memory, even forty-years later; and with only 54-hours on the ground it remains the longest SOG mission I ever participated in.

After Action Report

Upon landing on the airstrip, we were greeted by many of the Americans assigned to FOB 1, including the camp commander, Major Snell. This was a tradition, which existed because of the close bonds of friendship between the men of SOG and everyone's knowledge of the dangerous trips across the border. The first to greet me this day was my good friend and fellow SF Medic, Ron Romancik. He shook my hand and then handed me an ice cold beer. That one lasted a matter of seconds, as I sucked it down in an attempt to rehydrate. A second followed from the camp engineer and my roommate Ken Cryan. After thanking the pilots and crew chiefs for our safe return and shaking a lot more hands of friends and war brothers, we watched as the other choppers landed and the rest of ST Idaho unloaded. With everyone back, we all started walking back toward the front gate. As I passed Major Snell, he asked how it went and said that we would talk more after the team had some special chow.

Another nice tradition at FOB 1 was that the returning team was fed a nice steak dinner in the mess hall, no matter what time of day or night the return. After a quick shower and change, we met for our steaks. What a treat after eating rice, raisins, and peanuts for a few days. The camp chef was a Vietnamese gentleman who had learned to cook while working for the French during their war in Vietnam. He was a fabulous cook and served up the best food that I had while in the military. As we ate, we discussed the mission and the strange landing on the old Ashau airstrip.

After our meal, Tim, Glenn and I walked up to the S2 office for our de-briefing. Here we reported what we had seen and heard, turned over the film from our camera, and answered a lot of questions. Before leaving S2, we were told that something was brewing near Khe Sanh and that we should ready the team for travel to and launch from FOB 3.

After stopping at the team house and informing Mister Tu to ready the team for travel, we stopped by the Green Beret Lounge for a cold one. We were treated to a few rounds by the other One Zero's who had gathered there and answered their questions concerning our mission. Later, I retired to my "hooch" to catch up on some sleep.

Men of FOB 1 standing tall

Bright Light

Decades later…In the winter of 2004, I was having dinner with my wife Mary and son Joshua in a restaurant in Rhode Town on the island of Tortola, in the British Virgin Islands. At the table next to us was a couple, about our age, who struck up a conversation with us. Somehow, the conversation turned to Vietnam and the man we were talking to seemed quite knowledgeable about SOG and our secret mission in Vietnam. The information had just recently been declassified when the President awarded SOG a presidential Unit citation. No books about our operations had been published prior to this meeting and his knowledge of SOG was pretty extensive. He gave us only a first name and denied serving in the military. We were taking pictures of our family dinner in this little restaurant and he always managed to cover his face so that he could not be identified in the photos. I believe that he could have been CIA or a military intelligence officer of some sort.

During the conversation, he asked if I had met a man named Chuck Tobias who lived on the island. When I told him that I hadn't, he gave me the man's telephone number explaining that I should give the man a call and introduce myself before I left Tortola. Furthermore, he explained that Mr. Tobias was a Canadian citizen who had flown fast movers (F4 Phantoms) for the US Marines, and that he had been shot down over Laos in 1965. After spending several days on the ground, Mr. Tobias had been rescued by a SOG team on a Bright Light (rescue mission).

I had been on two Bright Light missions during 1968 and so I was quite interested in hearing the man's story. When I called, he was quite busy with business matters, but called me back before the day was out. I told him of my service with MACV SOG and he explained his crash and subsequent rescue. Furthermore, he explained how he had earned an engineering degree after leaving the service and had invented some sort of equipment for fighter aircraft. He then purchased the rights to Passer's Rum from the British Navy, and then opened a chain of restaurants in the Islands and one in Ft Lauderdale. His restaurants, named Pusser's, serve great food and drink, including their exclusive rum concoction known as the "Painkiller." It was very interesting to talk to a man rescued from deep within Laos by my brother warriors.

Bright Lights, Big City

SOG rescue mission's codenamed Bright Lights, were the most dangerous missions of all. The team was being inserted in an area where another team had been killed or captured, or where a plane had been shot down behind enemy lines. The enemy always knew that someone would be coming soon to look for those missing men. It was the American's value of human life and the sincere desire not to leave anyone behind that drove the men of SOG to readily volunteer for such dangerous work.

I can still remember the big Texas shit eating grin on the face of my One Zero, SFC Glen O. Lane, as he ducked through the low doorway to my hooch. Glenn was a pleasant, friendly man who would not be out of place in a ten gallon hat, western shirt, jeans, and boots with a six gun slung low on his hip. He was from Odessa, Texas and spoke with the drawl of Texas. He was a thirty-seven year old "lifer" who had spent time with Special Forces around the world. He was an experienced One Zero; and I learned a lot from him while I served as his One One on ST Idaho. This day, he had come looking for me not to have a beer, but to give me an early warning of a mission that we were now on standby for. With the grin as big as Texas never leaving his face, Glen said "get your boots shined because we are going to visit Uncle Ho." When I sat there with a confused look on my face, Glen explained that two Navy pilots had been shot down over North Vietnam and that we were going to look for them. He said that the wingmen had seen them bail out and that they had observed their parachutes opening. He also told me that the crash sites were only 11 kilometers (6.8 miles) from the outskirts of Hanoi. His reference to Uncle Ho referred to Ho Chi Minh, who was the Communist revolutionary president of the Peoples Republic of Vietnam at the time.

Although the mission was deemed urgent by the Secretary of the Navy and the Pentagon, it took several days to gather the necessary assets and to coordinate the logistical aspects of the mission. During those days, we were on standby and continued our training regime, and packing and repacking our gear for the mission. Finally, the American team members from Spike Team Idaho and the other team were called to the S2 office for a briefing on the mission. The snappy, young S2 officer pulled back the red curtain marked "Top Secret," revealing a map we had not seen before on this wall. It was a military topographical map of Northern Laos and North Vietnam. The officer explained the mission, pointing to the launch site, a refueling site, and the approximate location of the downed pilots. He gave the names and ranks of the pilots who we were looking for. He also issued each of us a little book in a plastic sleeve. The text, therein, was written in Vietnamese and Laotian and explained that we were Americans on a rescue mission and that we had been separated from our aircraft and were seeking assistance back to the border of Laos. The books were stamped with some sort of official seal from Laos and had a colored picture of an American Flag inside the front cover. Inside each sleeve were also five, crisp, green $100 US dollar bills. The young officer explained that the money was to pay our ransom or to pay for assistance in reaching the border, should we be separated from the group. It was unusual to see green American money in Vietnam, since the military was required to use MPC (military payment certificates) or the local Vietnamese currency.

The S2 officer informed us that we would be picked up by a C130 Blackbird at the Phu Bai Marine Airfield and flown to an Air Force Base at NKP (Nakhon Phanom), Thailand. He said that we would receive further briefing from the Air force when we arrived in Thailand. Our Commanding officer, Colonel Snell, had been in the briefing room and he stood up to address the group. He told us of the importance, as well as the dangerous nature of the mission. He stated that we could be shot down and/or captured and that there was nothing that could be done to rescue us. The Colonel then asked the group if any of us wanted to stay behind. There was no response from the room and so the Colonel bid us farewell.

The teams were assembled and loaded on a Deuce and a Half and driven South on Route One to the Marine Base and the Airfield. The truck drove across the tarmac to the waiting Blackbird, which already had its engines running. The guard motioned for us to go aboard and we were greeted at the top of the ramp by a funny, little guy in unmarked jungle fatigues. He looked too chubby, his sandy colored hair too long, and his uniform too clean to be a military. It turned out that he was some sort of ultra spook with the latest and greatest radio, capable of communication with Washington, D.C. or more likely, CIA headquarters at Langley Air Force Base.

After we got settled into the web seats along both sides of the aircraft, we taxied out and took off for the approximate one hour flight to NKP (Nakhon Phanom, Thailand) . Along the way, we painted on our camouflage and joked about visiting Hanoi and spending the green money. By the time we landed at NKP, it was late in the day and we were all ready to be inserted into North Vietnam. The problem was that the Air force apparently was not aware of our arrival, which left us stranded on the tarmac for about an hour.

Spike Team (ST) Idaho on Airstrip at NKP 1968

After about an hour sitting on the hot tarmac, Glen Lane flagged down a passing truck and bummed a ride for all 25 of us to the Base NCO club. That made perfect sense to me, as here we were, a very heavily armed band of strangers in a strange land, awaiting our flight on an ultra secret mission to rescue our fellow Americans from our Communist enemy, and we were headed to the NCO club for a cold beer or two. What could be more relevant to our "forgotten" band than to share a cold one on a hot day?

We loaded into the back of our "limousine" and were driven across the tarmac and the sprawling base to the NCO club. Surely here, this scary band could find answers to their every question and a cold drink to pass the time. As we walked into the noisy club, with 200-300 Americans in civilian clothing seated at tables, and a band playing on the well apportioned stage, suddenly silence fell over the room as every head turned to stare at the handsome lads who just crashed the party. As we pulled three tables together and seated ourselves around them, I had never felt as such a spectacle in my life. Lane, in his normal sense of humor, stated that no one was going to be asking any of us to dance so we might as well get drunk. He hailed a bargirl to order drinks for the table, but was interrupted by a big guy who introduced himself as the clubs manager. He VERY politely asked us to come outside for a talk, knowing full well that if a fight were to break out, that we, the strangers, were going to prevail since we were the only ones with assault rifles, hand grenades, knives, etc. And so, we, with parched throats, stood in unison and headed toward the exit. Once again, silence fell over the room as all turned to watch us be escorted out of the building.

When we got back in the sunlight, we were greeted by uniformed Air Police (AP). Everyone calmly explained to us that no weapons were allowed on the base and especially not in the club. We were asked the nationality of our indigenous team members and when we reported Vietnamese and Nungs, it was explained that bringing armed foreign nationals into Thailand was very likely an international incident. Lane briefly explained why were there and the AP said that he would have to check that out, but until our story was checked out, we would have to come with him. We were then loaded in the back of two windowless blue vans (AP Paddy wagons) and driven a short distance through the base. When the rear doors opened, we found ourselves inside a compound with double 12 foot high, chain link fences with coils of barbed razor wire on top. Shoot… here we were, good old American boys trying to do something good for the Navy and being held POW on an US Air Force base.

The APs escorted all of us into a sort of bunkhouse (read… holding cell) within the small enclosure. The cement block building was nice and clean, but had bars on the windows and sort of resembled a jail. The young airman suggested that we should all turn over our weapons so that they could be locked up, but SFC Lane explained that was just not going to happen. The guards then told us to make ourselves comfortable and closed the big steel doors behind them as they set out to check on our story.

About a half-hour later, the door creaked open and the APs came in, accompanied by an Air Force Captain who introduced himself as the "officer of the day." He apologized for not having met us on our arrival, but explained that the base was basically closed for the weekend and no one expected our arrival on a Sunday afternoon. He had confirmed our story through his chain of command and told us that we would be briefed at 0800 hrs the following morning. He told us that food would be served to us in an adjacent room, but that only the Americans in our group were free to go to the NCO club or anywhere else we chose on base. He explained that bringing armed foreigners into Thailand was, indeed, a problem and that the fewer people that saw our teammates, the better. This information was reluctantly explained to the teams through Hiep and they seemed to accept it better than we did. After all, these men would fight beside us, spill their blood with us, and perhaps even die with us. Their retention in this detention center was not appreciated by any of us.

After the long, hot frustrating day, the call of the NCO club beckoned. After settling the teams in for the night, the six of us left our rucksacks, web gear and CAR 15s behind with the teams and headed for the NCO club. We were still a scary looking bunch in our blackened, sterile jungle fatigues soaked in mosquito and leech repellant. None of us had shaved in the days that we were on standby, and our beards and unconventional narrow brimmed flop hats made us appear as a group of renegades (which I guess we were).

The NKP base could have been located in North Carolina or some other location stateside. The buildings, paved streets, signs etc. appeared as any of the other military bases I had visited while in the US. Nothing reminded me of being near a war zone or the military bases in South Vietnam.

When we arrived at the club, we found our way to an empty table to the right of the stage where a band was playing loud country and western music. We took our seats and hailed the waitress. Glenn ordered a round of Tiger Beer for the table. When the waitress returned, he attempted to pay her with MPCs from Vietnam and she said, "no good, need real money." After a brief pause, he reached in his pocket and pulled out the little plastic case with the book and his ransom money in it. He pulled out one of the $100 US bills and asked the waitress if that was real enough. She smiled with a huge grin, showing off a number of gold front teeth that flashed in the low lighting.

She said, "You get lots beer for that!" Lane responded, "Good, bring us six more." The Tiger Beers were a quarter a piece and I think that we polished off the hundred dollars between the beer and a few of the club's pizzas.

As we sat there "quenching our thirst", our table was approached by an Army SFC wearing jungle fatigues and a green beret with the flash of the Fifth Special Forces Group. I don't recall his name, but he introduced himself as the SOG liaison officer at NKP. He said that he had gotten word that our arrival had caused quite a stir. He pulled up a chair and shot the shit about SF, Phu Bai, Nha Trang, Ft Bragg, and all of the other stuff we had in common. We continued to drink beer and a few of the guys had stacked some of the empties in a pyramid in the center of the table that was now about ten cans high. The liaison officer asked what kind of weapons we were carrying and we all pulled out our concealed side arms. He had been referring to our weapons on the mission, but was interested in the deadly array now on display on the table. There were 45s, Beretta 25 automatics, Browning High Powers,

Walther PPks, and the experimental 13mm rocket pistol that I was carrying. The rocket pistol caught his eye, and I answered his questions about the piece. It was very light, the size of the 45 and felt and looked like a toy. One of the guys said that he bet that I could not shoot the top can off the beer can pyramid with that "flash Gordon gun." Not one to turn my back on a challenge, I waited for the band to start again, took aim and shot the can off the pile in the crowed club. The weapon had no loud report like a normal pistol and only a few people nearby suspected anything out of the ordinary as the side ports flashed fire and the can went flying. The trajectory of the round took it through the can and into the ceiling of the club. It was suggested at this point that we should pack up our pistols and return to the rest of the teams. When we got outside, the liaison officer said that he would be picking us up and driving us to the briefing in the morning; and that since the mission was such high priority, the Camp Commander, an Air Force General would be conducting the briefing.

We were up early and had breakfast with the teams and explained that we were going to the briefing and would return shortly. Our ride arrived and we were driven across the base to the headquarters building. I was impressed with how much this military base in northern Thailand looked as though it could have been stateside. The layout and the buildings had that American military look, and there really was nothing that would have made you think that you were in a foreign country.

The headquarters building was a big, one-story brick building, which we entered through the lobby. An airman was waiting to lead us through the hallways to the well appointed briefing/conference room. I felt very out of place sitting in one of the high-back leather chairs while dressed in my war suit. None of us had shaved for four or five days and our black-dyed, mosquito repellant soaked uniforms certainly did not match the official feel of this place. We were joined in the room by four Air Force officers in flight suits. These were the helicopter pilots who were assigned to fly us into North Vietnam. We were also surprised to see the funny, little guy in the new green jungle fatigues that we had not seen since arriving at the NKP airstrip. He took a seat by himself at the back of the room.

The room was called to attention as an Air Force Colonel and General in Class A uniforms entered the room. The officers introduced themselves and apologized for the confusion on our arrival. They explained that the powers in Washington were apparently undecided about sending Americans on the ground in North Vietnam and that we had arrived at NKP while the politicians were still trying to make up their minds. The decision to the men of SOG was simple **you never, ever leave a fellow warrior behind**.

The General repeated what we had heard from our S2 back in Phu Bai and filled us in on a lot of details. The two downed pilots were Navy officers who had been shot down to the North West of Hanoi while they were involved in bombing military targets as part of "Operation Rolling Thunder." In 1966, President Lyndon Johnson (LBJ) had lifted the ban on the bombing of Hanoi and Haiphong in accordance with the international "rules of war." His intent was to end the war sooner by demoralizing the enemy with the attacks on their homeland. The air raids were carried out by Air Force B52s flying from the US base in Guam, as well as by Navy fighter bombers off aircraft carriers in the Gulf of Tonkin.

F4 Phantom dropping 500 pound bombs (US Airforce photo)

The pilots that we were looking for had been flying F4 Phantom fighter bombers from the aircraft carrier USS Coral Sea. Their planes had been shot down by surface to air missiles (SAMs) to the northwest of Hanoi and their wingmen had seen their parachutes deploy as they ejected from their aircraft. We were familiar with the Phantoms as they often were the planes that came to the rescue of a team on the ground. We had received assistance from Phantoms flown by both Navy and Marine pilots while in South Vietnam and Laos; and now it was our turn to render assistance.

The General explained that the mission was extremely dangerous and that we would probably not be rescued if we were shot down. He explained that it almost took an act of Congress to have us flown in to attempt recovery of the pilots, and that acknowledgement of our armed invasion of North Vietnam was not a political situation that our government was willing to face. This is why we were given the little plastic sleeves with the Escape and Evasion packets written in several languages and the $500 that we were given to bribe our way to a friendly border. The General also explained that the area all around Hanoi was heavily fortified with SAM and antiaircraft sites, and that the sky surrounding the enemy capitol were patrolled by Soviet built MIG 21s.

The General turned the briefing over to the colonel who was the S2 officer. The Colonel explained the logistics of the mission. We would be flown to the area where the wingman saw the parachutes open in two Air Force Sikorsky Jolly Green Giant helicopters. These helicopters were from the Air Force Search and Air Rescue, and were equipped with titanium armor plating and a high speed winch with a jungle penetrator. We would watch for the parachutes, panels, or signal mirrors. We were to go on the ground only if we detected the presence of the missing pilots. While on the ground, we were not to engage the enemy except in self-defense. Our Jolly Greens would be escorted by one A1E Skyraider who would help direct our search and give us some limited air support. Our flight path would take us from NKP to a CIA refueling site #51 on the border between Northern Laos and North Vietnam. From the refueling site, we would fly along the high mountain ranges (up to

9,000 ft) to the Northwest of the city. It was hoped that the mountains would shield our slow moving helicopters from enemy radar and offer some sort of cover from the MIGs. The pilots were ordered not to put us on the ground unless we had positively located the pilots and only then if they had reasonable belief that we would be able to get the pilots out without a major firefight. We were instructed to bring back a hand or the head of the pilot if, for some reason, we were not able to recover the whole body, so that a positive identification could be made. He also made it clear that the final word on the insertion would be made by the lead chopper pilot and would be based on the weather, the chance of success, and the danger to the team and the aircraft.

We were dismissed from the briefing and told to recover our equipment, assemble the teams, and that we would be transferred from the security compound to waiting Jolly Greens. As we left the briefing, one of the NCOs said that he hoped he had enough of the ransom money left to pay for his

ticket out. We all got a good laugh out of that comment, remembering the beer consumption from the night before. When we returned to the security compound, the teams were already suited up and ready for the mission. We donned our web gear and ruk sacks, grabbed our weapons and headed for the airstrip.

Jolly Green Giant, Air Force photo

The Mission

We boarded the waiting helicopters with the first twelve man team in the first bird and ST Idaho in the second. The helicopters were manned by a crew of four men consisting of pilot, co-pilot, crew chief, and air rescue specialist. We all took seats in the webbed seats along the walls and awaited takeoff. As the choppers lifted off for the long flight, we applied our camouflage face paint in preparation for getting on the ground in North Vietnam.

We passed the hours looking at the jungle and mountains passing by below us. I was impressed by the vastness of the undeveloped areas of jungle and mountains. After flying almost due north for about two hours, the crew chief told us to strap ourselves in because we were making an unscheduled stop due to some sort of mechanical problem with our Jolly Green. We were bounced around a little as the helicopter autorotated in for a rather hard landing in a good sized opening in the jungle. The clearing was filled with wild grass and vines and the tree line was about 75-100 yards in all directions. As soon as we recovered from the abrupt stop, we exited the aircraft and formed a defensive perimeter around the chopper. The second chopper landed nearby and the other team also formed a perimeter. This was one of the maneuvers that we had practiced over and over again back on the FOB 1 airstrip. The purpose was to protect the chopper from attack until it could be airborne once again. As soon as we formed the perimeter, one of the young Vietnamese troops fired his M79 grenade launcher toward the tree line. There was no target and the new man received a tongue lashing from the Vietnamese team leader, Mr. Tu. This was once again an international incident. An armed invasion of the Sovereign Country of Laos by foreign nationals would be hard to explain. Luckily, within fifteen or twenty minutes, the problem with our bird was repaired and we were off flying north once again.

The other thing of interest that happened while we were on the ground was when the funny, little guy got off the aircraft and had two of the men help him spread out a long wire (doublet) antenna, which he attached to his radio set. He was then tapping away, sending Morse code over his secret, little radio to some unknown receiver. We could only speculate who he was and what his job was on this mission.

After perhaps another hour flying over Northern Laos, we spotted an area with a small airstrip beside a village of rustic, bamboo buildings. The surrounding area was scarred with hundreds of bomb craters on the rugged hilly terrain. We were told by the crew chief that this was refueling site 51 and that we should get ready to land. After a much smoother landing, we unloaded to stretch our legs, but the Vietnamese were instructed to stay on the aircraft to avoid any further political incidents. The small village was home to Hmong, small in size and an ancient cultured people who lived in the mountains of Laos. The CIA had recruited them to support the US in its fight against the Pathet Lao (the communists aligned with North Vietnam). The Hmong were eager to assist because they were routinely abused by the communist stealing their food and provisions. As the crew, assisted by a few Hmong, hand pumped fuel from 55-gallon drums into the thirsty choppers, we wandered through the village and down the airstrip to a Russian biplane that had been shot down with an M16 from an Air America chopper. The plane was upside down next to the runway and was in pretty good shape, for having been shot down. The plane had an open pipe about four inches in diameter welded through the floor, between the seats, and it was explained that this allowed the pilot to drop his rustic bombs through the pipe onto his target below. We were told that the Russian pilot had been badly injured in the incident and had been hauled as a POW by the Air America chopper the previous day.

When the tanks were full and our lone "Hobo" (A1E Skyraider) appeared overhead, we were off again. This time our flight took us to the East over some mountains and the border of North Vietnam. After pulling away from the refueling site, the bomb craters diminished until only jungle and mountains remained. Before long, we were flying along a deep valley with jagged peaks on our port side. We kept watching for signs of the downed pilots until we came to low lying clouds that filled the valley below us. As we flew along just above the clouds, we continued to watch the steep slope and jagged cliffs on our port side. There was a certain level of apprehension in the air as we skipped along the dense clouds waiting for some sign of the pilots as darkness began to fill the valley below. The crew chief was alerted by the pilot to have us all look forward to see the glow of the lights of Hanoi in the evening sky. As we were looking at the lights, we were told to hang on because we were taking evasive action from enemy aircraft. As we looked out the starboard windows, we saw our Hobo escort dive down through the clouds with our Jolly Greens soon following. Before the sky was completely obstructed by the thick clouds, we looked up and saw the reason for the sudden radical maneuvers. There, high above us was a lone MIG still lit by the fading sunlight. He did not apparently see us and continued onward as we disappeared below the clouds.

After a short ride just below the clouds, we were informed that the mission had been scrubbed by higher authority and that we were to return to NKP. We were told that the SAM and antiaircraft gun sites along with patrolling MIGs and the adverse weather were the reason that the mission was cancelled. As the helicopters turned 180 degrees and headed back toward the border, we observed the lights of a few villages and military compounds in the valley below. We strapped ourselves in and hoped that the pilot would fly us home without encountering any more MIGs, or fly us into the mountainside in the dark cloudy night.

We were all disappointed that we were not able to find and perhaps, rescue the fly boys but were happy to find ourselves flying toward the "friendly skys" of Laos, Thiland, and South Vietnam. And so ended my first Bright Light mission. My next Bright Light mission was my last mission in Vietnam; and was an effort to rescue ST Idaho, the same team that I had been assigned to during this first Bright Light.

Khe Sanh to Saigon

With only two days to catch our breath, St Idaho was off again. This mission was farther to the north in the hilly region surrounding Khe Sanh. Intelligence reports had noted a significant increase in enemy activity in the area. The Marines in Khe Sanh had been getting hit by rocket and artillery fire of increasing intensity over recent weeks; and aircraft had noted an increase in truck and troop traffic along the North South highway from North Vietnam. The Pentagon wanted a closer look and a description of the traffic travelling Vietnam highway 9 under cover of darkness. ST Idaho was one of the only teams available at the time to take that look.

We loaded up for the flight to Khe Sanh. The pilots followed Highway One, north of Phu Bai, over the village of Phu Luong and along this busy route, skirted by rice paddies. It was surreal to look down on the black pajama clothed people in their traditional pointed, straw coolie hats working the paddies with their yoked water buffalo. It did not seem that such peaceful endeavors could be taking place in a country torn by war. The busy Highway One was not in any way similar to the Pacific Coast Highway 101(PCH) back in California, but for a few brief moments, I relived memories of my life along the PCH. My travels on the Pacific Coast Highway were in woody station wagons loaded with surfboards, in 55 Chevys, and Model A Fords that belonged to good friends Chuck Bell and Steve Garrett. But, here I was flying along a highway where three wheeled Lambrettas carrying way too many passengers, some with baskets of chickens or pigs lashed on top, passed each other surrounded by motor scooters, military vehicles, and foot traffic. Some pedestrians here carried their belongings on yokes over the shoulders with hanging baskets on either side. This highway, I decided, had a lot more personality than the Pacific Coast Highway of the western United States. Its travelers stopped here and there for a snack or perhaps for pac time (siesta). Pac time was the traditional afternoon rest common in this hot climate.

The road led us to the bridge over the Perfume River and over the Provincial capital of Hue. We had visited this beautiful city of about 117,000 on several occasions. It was here that we bought 100-pound blocks of ice to chill our beer and where, to the chagrin of the Marines who guarded the area, we occasionally visited the ice cream parlor run by an old French couple. The proprietors name was Pierre (of course) and he would tell us tales of the French colonial days as we enjoyed the homemade ice cream, which he had produced. The city had some beautiful buildings dating back as far as the Ming Dynasty in 1600. Flying over the city was a different experience and the hustle and bustle faded as we continued to the Northwest.

Perfume River, Hue, Vietnam 1968, Romancik photo

As the city disappeared behind us, the jungle carpeted the land. Occasional glimpses of a road or village would appear and in some places, the jungle was broken by the green of fields and open land. We went through a pass with beautiful, green mountains on both sides and open pasture like land in the valley between. We spotted a group of deer grazing in the field near a road. Hiep identified the road as Vietnam Highway 9, a major route entering Vietnam from Laos which would have been highly travelled by invading forces from North Vietnam had it not been for the Special Forces Camp at Lang Vei and the Large Marine Base at Khe Sanh, which were built along the roadside. Within weeks of this mission, the North Vietnamese would overrun the Special Forces camp at Lang Vei and the seventy day siege of Khe Sanh would begin.

Khe Sanh was on a plateau surrounded by hilly terrain. It was only a short distance from the base to the DMZ to the north, or Laos to the West. Many of the hilltops around the plateau were controlled by the Marines. Famous battles were fought here and many brave young Americans died in this place. Some questioned the value of holding Khe Sanh through the siege, but I believe the will of the Communists was broken here. Had it not been for the shenanigans of our politicians back home the war in Vietnam would have ended differently.

My first view of the Khe Sanh plateau was of thousands of bomb craters, in long strings, created by the B52 sorties (arc lights). I then saw the airstrip on the northern edge of the Marine base. At the end of the runway were the burnt out remains of a C130 Hercules, which had been hit a few days earlier while delivering supplies to the Marines. We landed near the remains of two Slicks (UH1s) also destroyed by enemy fire. We were greeted by someone from FOB 3 in an open ¾ ton truck. We quickly loaded up and headed for FOB 3. The FOB was located directly across the Marine base, outside the wire, on the southwestern side. Travel through the Marine base was a real eye opener. Here, young Marines (who appeared no older than 18 or 19 years old) lived basically underground. The earth was red clay and the uniforms of the Marines had assumed the color of the earth in which they lived. The base was a lattice work of trenches and bunkers piled high with sandbags. The accommodations were much different than the "luxury accommodations" back at Phu Bai. I felt sorry for these young marines and very grateful for my hooch back at FOB 1.

FOB 3 was a base unto itself. It was constructed beyond the wire of the Marine base. It, too, had trenches from one hooch to another. I recall the dispensary being a walled tent with sandbags piled about four feet high around its perimeter. I remember meeting a few of the "locals," and hearing about the shelling at night and the sounds of the NVA digging trenches ever closer to the camps perimeter. I remember little else about our stay at FOB 3 other than a briefing at S2 and the Marine UH1 flying Lane out for a VR. When Lane returned and the chopper was refueled, we loaded the team and flew off into the late afternoon light. Our target was on the side of Co Roc Mountain near where Highway 9 crossed into Laos. Lane had found a great LZ which was densely covered with tall elephant grass. The spot was level enough and clear enough for the choppers to hover just above the blown over grass, while the team jumped in from the helicopters skids. The insertion went without enemy contact or other incident and Lane quickly moved us into the tree line for cover. The vegetation here was significantly different from that in the Ashau Valley and seemed somehow more lush and green. It was late in the day and so our first objective had to be to find a good defensive position for our RON. Within one hour, we had found a somewhat sheltered piece of ground large enough for us to spread out for the night. From this RON, we could also catch a glimpse of Highway 9 to our north at about 300-400 yards.

On this night, Lane sensed that we were in a dangerous location and ordered the six of us to all remain on watch for the night. After we ate our meager rations, I gave each man a dexamyl capsule to help ward off sleepiness. Shortly after darkness fell, we began hearing traffic on the road. We could barely make out the shadowy images of what appeared to be trucks moving to the East. After an hour or so, we began to hear the distinctive sound of track vehicles moving through the night. This continued for some time and the information was passed on by radio relay. We kicked ourselves for not carrying a cumbersome starlight scope, which would have given us a better view of the vehicles as they passed by toward Lang Vei and Khe Sanh. In 1968, night vision equipment was large and heavy and nothing like the products commercially available today. After about 0100 hrs, the traffic had stopped and nothing more happened during the night.

Early the next morning, we observed an enemy patrol moving on the hillside behind us. Lane figured they were tracking us and moved the team quietly through thick undergrowth, toward the highway. Kirk called for immediate extraction and reported our location and direction of movement. As we broke from the edge of the tree line, we came into a clearing where the ground was all torn up and there were plenty of tracks from what we believed to be the tanks we heard the night before. As we were looking at the tracks, we heard the choppers coming up the valley and took cover to await their arrival. When we saw them coming, Lane popped a yellow smoke and stood waving his arms at the choppers. The Marines swooped down and we were aboard in an instant. As we lifted off, the enemy soldiers appeared on the tree line and began shooting their AK47s at us. We returned fire with our CAR 15s as we flew off to a safe altitude. The Marines flew us directly back to Phu Bai and landed at FOB 1. We were greeted not only by our friends from FOB 1, but also CCN commander Colonel Warren, who congratulated us on our successful mission and asked Lane which one of us was willing to fly with the indigenous team members down to Saigon to brief MACV. The Vietnamese were allowed to go home to celebrate Lunar New Year (Tet) with their families and the Colonel wanted to make sure that they had an escort to ensure that there was no problem with their transportation. Lane said that he did not care to go and that I should go to Saigon with the team the following morning.

After cleaning up and storing our gear, we went to the mess hall for our traditional steak dinners. Following this, we were called to S2 for our debriefing. During the debriefing, Lane clearly described what we had heard and seen the night before to the S2 officer. The S2 officer said that we were surely mistaken because MACV knew that the North Vietnamese had no tanks. Lane, with our full support, respectfully disagreed with the officers about what we had heard and seen, but the officers insisted that what we had heard and seen were probably sounds and tracks from bulldozers used to repair Highway 9 after B52s had bombed it.

To Saigon

Travel between Phu Bai and Saigon in 1968, Vietnam was an adventure all by itself. We departed the FOB 1 airstrip by the familiar Kingbee and travelled south along Highway 1. This land was beautiful, covered in dense green and checkered with rice paddies. Picturesque thatched villages were sparsely scattered along the road and salt water estuaries intruded inland, spotted by netted fish traps on posts and the sampans used by the fishermen. As we approached Da Nang, we passed over Da Nang Harbor with a number of US Warships and one white painted hospital ship at anchor. Our trip had a layover in Da Nang which was the busiest airport in the world during 1968, where 55,000 flights took off and landed each month. As we came in for landing, we watched some "fast movers" (F-4 Phantom Jets), fully loaded with bombs taking off, using their afterburners to quickly gain altitude. We also saw cargo planes (C130s and C141s) taking off and landing on the parallel runways. My personal favorites to watch were the "Hobos" (Douglas A1E Skyraiders). These radial engine birds, in production since 1947, were flown by pilots from the US Air Force 1st SOS (Special Operations Squadron). As they taxied down the runway, the pilots would often slide back their glass canopy and their orange ascots would trail behind them in the breeze. These planes provided the best combat support for SOG teams on the ground in Laos. Their slower speed allowed them to drop napalm and bombs, or use their 20MM cannons to attack the enemy within yards of a team's position. I recall on one mission, a pilot rolling the plane upside down just over our position and we could see him saluting us from his cockpit. On a "Bright Light" mission to North Vietnam, it was a lone Hobo that escorted our helicopters from the Laotian border to within 11 Kilometers of Hanoi.

After a short wait on the busy tarmac, we were picked up by a vehicle from CCN headquarters and driven to a major intersection downtown. Here the Vietnamese team members unloaded and left to visit their relatives in the city. Hiep assured me that we would meet in the morning to continue our travels south to Saigon. I was then driven to a SOG safe house at 22 Lei Loy Street in Da Nang. This was the notorious House 22 where the men of SOG would stay overnight, while moving through Da Nang. It was an old, two story, French Villa with a high wall around the property and a guarded iron gate, which opened onto Lei Loy street. Everything a warrior needed for a relaxing night was available at "House 22." Each time I stayed here, it reminded me of the 1964 song by the Animals, "House of the Rising Sun." Not only were the villa and the surrounding buildings similar to those of the French Quarter in New Orleans, but the happenings here, with booze and prostitutes, were wild.

The following day, I was driven back to the Da Nang airport and to a guarded high security area where I found Hiep waiting for me. There were several "special" aircraft parked in this area, which were painted with black and dark green camouflage paint. There were two C130s and a C123 with the black paint parked here. Each had an armed guard standing near the open tailgates. These were the planes that we referred to as "Blackbirds", which provided much of the transportation of SOG teams on long range missions. On this particular day, Hiep and I were told to board one of the C130s. As we approached the aircraft, we were stopped by the guard who asked for our orders. I produced my Classified Courier Orders and after Hiep showed the guard his papers, we were allowed to climb aboard.

The Blackbirds were conventional US planes with some extraordinary modifications, beyond their unconventional paintjobs and lack of traditional markings. In this C130, there was an enclosed "secret" area about twelve square feet behind the cockpit. Although I was never inside the secret compartment, I had, on one occasion, caught a glimpse of a wide array of electronic equipment through an open doorway, and was told at some point on one of these flights, that the compartment contained highly classified radio listening, jamming, and communications equipment. I was also told that every time these planes took off, that coded information was sent directly to the pentagon. The pilot and crew appeared to be of Asian descent and were clothed in civilian clothing, like you would expect to see on any tourist to the tropics.

Hiep and I were the only passengers and the only cargo was a nice, shiny military Jeep being transported to Saigon for some unknown reason. These planes, designed for cargo and troop transport, were noisy and uncomfortable. We sat in the webbed seating, along the fuselage and facing the Jeep, which was tied down securely in the center of the cargo area. The flight was long, hot, and boring and I remember little of the flight other than Hiep inviting me to come to his parent's home in Saigon for the traditional Tet dinner. I told him that I would be honored, and so he gave me the address, telling me what time to arrive on the appointed evening.

After landing at Tan Son Nhut Airport in Saigon, I was driven by Jeep, directly to MACV headquarters for the debriefing. I was escorted into the well-fortified building and into a room with the walls covered with military maps. I was joined by a captain and a major, as well as a CIA analyst in civilian clothing who questioned me about the mission to CO Roc Mountain and, in particular, about the sounds and tracks which ST Idaho had observed in the target area. The officers, like those at FOB 1, said that I must have been mistaken, as there was no prior intelligence of the NVA having tanks south of the DMZ.

On February 7, 1968, just weeks after my meeting in Saigon, the Special Forces camp at Lang Vei was overrun by the NVA. The NVA had driven Soviet S-76 tanks through the wire and over the bunkers. Most of the Americans and indigenous personnel in the camp at the time were killed. A few survived by barricading themselves inside the command bunker. Many of the tanks were destroyed in the airstrikes that followed, as were hundreds of NVA while Puff the Magic Dragon (Code named Spooky). Spooky was a Douglas AC-47 with three mini-guns mounted on the port side(left side), each gun fired 100 rounds per second or an incredible 6,000 rounds per minute, with a mighty roar of the guns and the fact that every fourth round being a tracer, this "Dragon" spit its deadly fire on the enemy as it circled above, riddling the camp and surrounding area with hundreds of thousands of bullets.

The tanks, which were supplied by the Soviet Union, had been driven down from North Vietnam under cover of darkness and had been hidden under jungle canopy or in caves along the roadside during daylight hours. As far as I know, ST Idaho was the only team who had encountered the tanks before the Lang Vei massacre. The men of SOG risked their lives on every mission to gather intelligence, which could help prevent tragedies like Lang Vei from happening to friendly forces in Vietnam. Sometimes the S2 officers just could not bring themselves to believe what the teams had seen or heard, and the intelligence was, thereby, rendered useless.

Debriefing complete, I was driven from MACV headquarters to the SOG Safe house where I was scheduled to stay for three days. The safe house was another old, two story, French villa situated in a nice residential section of the city, only a few blocks off the notorious Tu Do Street. It was surrounded by a ten foot high wall with armed guards at the gate leading to the street. There were only a handful of other SOG personnel staying at the house. I befriended a Staff Sergeant who said that he was stationed in the Mekong Delta. We spent our time swapping stories from home, drinking Ba Mui Ba, "33" (the local beer) and playing chess.

On the night appointed, I had the guard hail a cab (an open Lambretta,) to take me to Hiep's home. The ride lasted about a half hour and was very interesting. The city of Saigon was a beautiful place, indeed, and it is no wonder that it had earned the nickname of "Paris of the Orient." There were tree lined streets with large villas, parks with statues, and beautiful old Buddhist shrines. The major roads were packed with refugees on foot and on motorbikes, fleeing the communists back in their native villages and towns. On that night, Saigon was still considered a safe haven, far from the "front lines" of war. That would all change the following day however, when the North Vietnamese army would invade Saigon on the first day of the Tet Offensive of 1968. For that night,however, there was peace and only the bustle of a busy city. The streets were crowded and both civilian and military police attempted to direct the traffic. The Saigon Cowboys (a nickname for tough or cool young men aboard their 50cc Hondas) cut in and out of traffic, often using the sidewalks to escape a traffic jam. Tu Do Street was alive with restaurants, bars and nightclubs, with brightly clothed young women beckoning passersby to come into their establishments and buy them a "Saigon Tea."

My ride continued on through the city to Hiep's house. When we pulled up in front of his house, I was greeted by a smiling Hiep and a few of his younger brothers on the front steps. Hiep had been raised as a Buddhist and had learned English while attending a French school in Saigon. Before serving with Special Operations Group, Hiep had served as an interpreter for the US Special Forces. His English was excellent and was accented with some of the slang of the American GI's with which he worked. Being invited to his home for dinner was a great honor for me, though I approached it as sort of a "stranger in a strange land."

My memories of that delightful visit remain vivid to this day. I remember being greeted by an elderly woman, Mrs. Kia Nguyen, who did not speak English, Hiep, and his younger brothers Tuan, Minh and Tam. Also gathered for the family celebration were Hiep's sister, Loan and her husband, Major Thuan Le of the Vietnamese Air Force. The gathering reminded me of my own family gatherings for Christmas or Thanksgiving. As we sat for the Tet dinner, I was given a chair at the end of the table opposite Major Le and was treated as an honored guest. I remember the laughter of the children as I attempted to eat this special meal with chop sticks and the kindness of Hiep's mother, Kia, who went to the kitchen, returning with the only fork in the house, bowing as she handed it to me. I thanked her and Hiep translated for me. As I remember, the meal consisted of Pho (Vietnamese beef and noodle soup), freshly baked French bread, and a Tet specialty that I shall never forget, called Banh Chung, a delicacy that my western palate did not enjoy, consisting of layers of pork, rice, and mung bean wrapped tightly in banana leaves and boiled for eight to ten hours. Both the taste and smell reminded me of spoiled meat and it was all I could do to get it down.

Hiep and his family were Buddhist; and Hiep had attended a French school in Saigon where he learned to speak English. Hiep narrowly escaped Vietnam with his family during the "Fall of Saigon" on April 30, 1975. He now lives in Texas with his family and owns and operates a pet shop. Also living in Texas are Hiep's Brothers and Sister, and her husband. I am happy that my friends were able to escape the fall of Saigon and the re-education camps that followed.

Tet Offensive 1968

After having dinner with Hiep and his family, I caught a ride back to the SOG safe house and joined a few of the temporary residents for drinks on Tu Do Street. On that evening of January 30, 1968, we had no idea that the city had been infiltrated by thousands of General Giaps NVA troops. The NVA had disguised themselves as refugees or South Vietnamese soldiers on leave for the holiday; and they had drifted into the city over the past weeks. Their weapons had been smuggled into the city in coffins and produce wagons, and they had come to "liberate" the city of Saigon. As we partied that night, it is possible that we rubbed elbows with the enemy in the crowded bars of Tu Do Street. We wore civilian clothing and carried concealed weapons, but our "big guns" were back in the safe house. I was carrying a Browning 9mm pistol under my shirt and a 25 cal "wallet pistol" in my pocket. I never felt threatened in any way that evening and had no idea that all hell was about to break out in the city the next day.

I awoke at the safe house with a bit of a hangover. After I got up and took a few standard issue APCs, I went down to the parlor to continue the prior day's game of chess. While pondering my next move, I heard the unmistakable sound of UH1 helicopters flying directly overhead and firing their rockets at some nearby target. After running up to the roof of the villa and seeing the choppers circling and clouds of smoke only a few blocks away, we decided to go investigate. We grabbed our web gear and CAR 15s and headed out the gate of the compound in search of answers. The safe house (villa) was located on a wide alley like street with other large villas on both sides. Most were surrounded by high concrete or stucco walls with wrought iron gates opening onto the alleyway. The architecture, wrought iron and even the smell of the place reminded me of the French Quarter in New Orleans.

A few villas down from our gate, we encountered a group of Americans in civilian clothing standing in the alley and looking in the direction of the smoke. We asked them if they knew what was going on; and they told us that the North Vietnamese had infiltrated the city and attacked the US Embassy,

Tan Son Nhut Airport, and several other targets in the city. The men identified themselves as employees of Air America and being unarmed, chose not to join my comrade and I on our excursion toward the action.

My friend and I slowly made our way down the alleyway for about 500 meters where we approached a major cross street. I observed two men dressed in fatigues and armed with AK-47s crouching behind a low wall and firing at passing helicopters. I shouldered my weapon and ended their military careers with a single shot to the side of each man's head. Almost immediately, a couple of Marines in flak jackets and steel helmets came around the corner and asked us to identify ourselves. We told them who we were and where we had walked from and they told us that we should return to our safe house because the city was under attack and that it was not safe for us to be on the street. Taking the Marines advice, we headed back up the alleyway toward our villa. On passing the Air America group, we were invited in for a beer. As we drank our beers, with the sounds of gunfire and explosions down the street, these guys briefed us on what was going on around South Vietnam: they told us how the North Vietnamese had simultaneously attacked most of the major cities and military bases in South Vietnam. They said that Phu Bai and Hue were among the attacked locations, but were uncertain as to the extent of the casualties or damage. They said that Tan Son Nhut Airport had suffered damage and that all non combat flights were grounded. I was troubled that ST Idaho was scattered from FOB 1 in Phu Bai through Da Nang to Saigon and Cholon. What would happen to my friends in Phu Bai and how would our indigenous team members survive unarmed and on the streets? I thought about the predicament long and hard and felt trapped in that old, French villa in Saigon. Perhaps a wiser man would have felt fortunate to sit out the largest offensive of the Vietnam War in the relative safety of this French villa, with ample food and drink, but I felt trapped here and attempted every day for transport back to FOB 1. That transport would not happen for a week and a half.

After the fighting had died down in Saigon, I again made the trip down the alleyway to the intersection where I had encountered the Marines and the enemy insurgents. As I entered the main street, I saw hundreds of bodies lined up on the sidewalk. There were dead enemy combatants in uniform, some in the classic black pajamas and straw hats of peasants, and some in little more than loin cloths. I do not know what the final death toll was, but could see at a glance that the enemy had lost a lot of men in Saigon.

History shows that the North Vietnamese suffered horrific losses in their attack on the South. I have read that the NVA and VC death toll for Saigon and Tan Son Nhut was over 1,700 killed and 7,000 captured with an unknown number wounded. The numbers were similar throughout South Vietnam and I understand that General Giap, who commanded the invasion, thought that this would be the end for North Vietnam's "liberation" of the Southland. Little did Giap know at the time that the American peace movement and the weak-kneed, crooked politicians in Washington would hand over South Vietnam without a fight just a few years later in March of 1973. I lost a lot of faith in my government and in my fellow Americans when I saw my Nation abandon our friends in South Vietnam to the re-education camps and executions carried out by the invading army of the North. I am thankful that a few of those Vietnamese whom I knew best were able to escape a fate worse than death on the last choppers and planes departing Saigon in April of 1975. Memories of the others haunt me to this day and I often wonder what became of Tu, Ha, Sau and the others. I will never forget them and the battles for freedom that we fought together in their beautiful country.

Whatever happened to men like John F. Kennedy who once said,

"Let every nation know, whether it wishes us well or ill, that we shall pay any price, bear any burden, meet any hardship, support any friend, oppose any foe, to assure the survival and the success of liberty."

What happened to the integrity and grit of America?

After the fighting had pretty much ended in Saigon, we took advantage of our "Classified Courier Orders" and hailed a cab for a place that I only knew as the Chief's Club, a four or five story building off Tu Do Street, which I was told was run by the Navy Chiefs Association. On the roof was a canopied bar, a live band and a dance floor. There were a lot of pretty Vietnamese women all dressed up, ready to drink and dance with the visiting NCOs, so we drank and danced that night under a starlit Saigon. I learned later that all the women had apartments on the lower floors and that this was really a five-story brothel. What a war.

When we left the "Chief's Club" in the wee hours, we were stopped by the Military Police (MP) demanding to know what we were doing on the street. It seemed that there was a curfew in effect and that the MP's just could not understand why three drunken Americans in civilian clothing were on the street at this hour. We produced our orders, were given a ride back to the safe house in the MP's Jeep, and warned to stay off the streets past curfew on future nights.

The demeanor of this ancient city was forever changed by the communist invasion. It is estimated that two million civilian refugees had fled their villages and towns for the "safety" of the capital city. The population did not shrink again until the communists came back in 1975 and renamed the city Ho Chi Minh City. People were ordered back to the countryside to work the fields and rice paddies, while many others were sent to the "work camps" which were called re-education camps. Most Vietnamese who escaped by chopper or boat still refer to the city as Saigon and I, for one, shall always remember the city as a free Saigon.

After about a week and a half, MACV got tired of me pestering them about getting back to Phu Bai, and so they put me on an old civilian airliner. "What a trip", the plane was an old DC 3, constructed sometime between 1920-1930. The flight was one of the first civilian flights to leave Saigon, after Tet and all of the other passengers were Vietnamese government officials flying north to check on their families in the besieged cities to the north. In those days, there was no public communication system in South Vietnam; and the chaos of the offensive had cut off families and friends. I spent the entire flight looking out of the window at the bombed out villages and hamlets along the way. The old DC-3 rolled to a stop on the runway in Nha Trang. I was able to catch a ride on a De Havilland Canada C7-A "Caribou", which was dropping cargo at some remote airfield and continuing on to Da Nang. This would be my only flight in a Caribou and proved to be quite an experience.

The C7-A aircraft was designed for short runway landings and takeoffs, and the cargo delivery was to just such a place; and although the destination runway was surrounded by high mountain cliffs on all sides, the Caribou seemed to float effortlessly down to a soft and very short landing. The cargo was quickly rolled out the back of the plane as we were rolling down the runway toward the high cliff in front of us. The Caribou seemed to lift off at a very low speed and effortlessly float upward missing the cliff by what seemed like a few feet. After a smooth flight of an hour or so, we landed in Da Nang. I contacted CCN(Command and Control North headquarters) and was transported to the familiar House 22.

I waited for four days in House 22 for a ride back to Phu Bai. I met other stranded men of SOG and learned of the loss of my friend and neighbor, James Leslie "Les" Moreland. Les was a Green Beret and was assigned to A-team 101 at Long Vei. There, 24 American Special Forces Personnel and 500 Montagnard CIDG (Civilian Irregular Defense Groups) lived in their fortified camp. On the night of February 6th, 1968 the camp was attacked by two NVA infantry battalions, two sapper companies, and two armored companies. The camp had been forewarned about the "possibility" of the NVA having tanks and had prepared by storing a supply of LAWs and extra rounds for their 106mm and 57mm recoilless rifles. The Americans were able to destroy a total of seven of the Soviet supplied PT-76 tanks, but the remaining five overran the camp. Seven Americans and two hundred of the Montagnards were killed, and an additional eleven Americans and seventy-five Montagnards who were wounded. Three Americans were taken prisoner and my friend Les was initially listed as MIA(Missing In Action). This Green Berets remains were identified in 2011 and are to be buried next to his parents in Alabama.

I was told that Les had been wounded on the first night of the battle with a gunshot wound to the head. He had been bandaged up and escorted back to the operations center, which was an underground bunker. The following day, after the camp had been overrun, Les was delirious from his brain injury and left the safety of the bunker to kill some "Commies." He was never seen alive again. His remains were recovered among the bodies (both friendly and enemy) strewn around the perimeter of the camp. I had met Les on a trip home between training classes at Ft. Bragg. His elderly, widowed mother lived in the town of Westminster, California, which is adjacent to my parent's home town in Huntington Beach.

On that trip, we met each other's families and went out for drinks on a few occasions. I was saddened by the loss of Les and remembered our night on Co-Roc Mountain listening to tracked vehicles on Highway 9. Both the horror of war and the value of SOGs recon work became more real to me that night. Les was not the only friend I would lose in Vietnam, but he was one of the first. I got little sleep that night thinking about what I had learned and unavoidably hearing someone "banging" a prostitute in the bunk bed next to mine.

The following day, an NCO arrived from Phu Bai who had finished his tour and was headed back to the States. He told me how FOB 1 had been attacked by the NVA with 122mm rockets and that several of the buildings had been destroyed. He said that some of the camps' civilian employees were taken POW by the NVA in Hue and were to be tried for "crimes against the people." We learned later that many such people were tried and killed by the communists and buried in mass graves. These NVA were the "peace loving people" embraced by Hanoi Jane Fonda, and the peace creeps back home. We, who served here, had a very different impression of these barbarians.

To this day, I consider Hanoi Jane and the peace creeps of the sixties and seventies as traitors worthy of nothing but dishonor. Their cries of protest echoed around the globe, encouraging our enemies, and finally led to our dishonorable withdrawal from Vietnam. Many fine Americans had given their lives to free the oppressed in South Vietnam; and their work was almost done before Walter Cronkite wrongly announced on national television in 1968 that; "we are losing the war in Vietnam."

Two days later, a CCN Jeep came to pick me up and take me to the airstrip for my ride back to Phu Bai. I climbed aboard one of the familiar Kingbee and finally headed north for <u>home</u>. I noted many new bomb craters and burned out villages along Highway 1, but the lush beauty of the land somehow remained. I saw fishermen tending their nets with four poled fish traps on one side of the highway, while on the other side, yoked water buffalo working the rice paddies, tended by villagers in black pajamas and the pointed straw hats.

When we arrived at FOB 1, the pilot made the traditional, steep 360-degree turn around the camp; and I noticed that the Cambodian mess hall and a few other buildings were razed to the concrete slabs on which they once stood. The old, French bunkers, the trenches, the 60-foot rappelling tower, and the mine fields all seemed unchanged. As we landed on the airstrip, I was greeted by Glenn Lane, Tu and Ha, who had got word of my return. Hiep had somehow caught a C130 that brought him directly from Saigon to the Marine airfield at Phu Bai the previous day. Lane told me not to get too comfortable because ST Idaho was scheduled for another target in the Ashau Valley the following day. He told me that our One Two, Tim Kirk, had been sent to Khe Sanh with a Hatchet Force to reinforce FOB 3 and rescue the survivors of A-team 101 at Lang Vei. I would not see Tim again until nearly fourth years later, in September of 2002 at a reunion of the men of the Special Operations Association in Las Vegas, Nevada.

Lane informed me that we would be traveling with some new guy on the radio and that there had been little time to train him with the team. After going to my hooch and checking all of my gear for the mission, I met Lane and the new man in the club for a beer. The new radio man was SSG (Staff Sergeant) Robert Owen. Lane informed us that the targets had become even more dangerous after TET, as many of the North Vietnamese regulars had run for sanctuary in Laos after getting a good ass kicking within the borders of South Vietnam. Our mission was to assess enemy strength in the Valley and to snatch a prisoner if we could.

The following morning, pilots reported 100% cloud cover over the target area, so the mission was rescheduled for the following day. This gave me additional time to catch my breath and visit with a few of my friends in the camp.

My roommate and closest friend at FOB 1 told me that he had tired of his position as the camp engineer and had volunteered to serve on an ST. He had been assigned to One Zero SSG Allen, and would be the "One One" on ST Alabama. My good friend and fellow medic Ron Romancik had been assigned to do away with the FOB 1 rat population. Another friend, Patrick Johnston, One Zero of ST New Jersey, was almost finished his tour in Vietnam and was headed home to the "World" in a few days I also had a beer with one of my mentors MSG Charlie Harper, patted Lady(the FOB 1 German Shepherd mascot) on the head, and threw an apple to "Andy the pig." It was a good day to remember at FOB 1... It's a peculiar thing when you are in a war, far from home, and you can remember many of the names of the people you met forty-years after the fact. Today, I meet people and cannot remember their names four minutes later.

At first light, ST Idaho gathered outside the team house for a quick inspection by Glenn Lane. Glenn knew the indigenous team members well, and he knew that they would be carrying the proper gear, ammunition, and food for the five-day mission. We carried two extra weapons (LAWs) on this mission in case we ran across any of the Soviet Tanks. I was to carry one at the rear and Ha was to carry one in the point position. Lane paid particular attention to Owen, checking the PRC 25 radio, his ammo supply, grenades, etc. When Lane was satisfied, we headed out the front gate and across the street to wait for the approaching Slicks. Within a few minutes, the Slicks circled the camp and landed in a huge cloud of dust. Idaho loaded into the first two choppers and a Special Forces chase medic, Bruce Johnston, loaded into the third. As soon as everyone was aboard, the helicopters took off and climbed to join our escort of three Marine UH-1 gunships armed with rocket pods and mini-guns. The prop wash from the rotors cooled us down as it blew through the open doorways. It felt good to be back in action with my team after being stuck in Saigon and Da Nang for two weeks.

As we approached the LZ, the gunships swooped down for a couple of low passes to see if they would draw any fire. When they climbed back to altitude, at perhaps 500ft above the jungle canopy, the first Slick, carrying Lane, Owen and Hiep flew down and hovered at about 100 ft above the dense underbrush of the LZ. The three men rappelled down nylon ropes and quickly set up a defensive perimeter as my chopper swooped down into position and the three of us also rappelled down. I was the last man to exit the chopper; and it apparently had risen a few feet, since I came to the end of my rope about ten feet above the ground and landed, as Lane put it, like a "sack of shit." Nothing was really hurt (but my pride) so the choppers left us in the hush of the Jungle.

The sounds of the rotors could still be heard in the distance as the team started to move off the LZ. All of a sudden, all hell broke loose. We were receiving fire from three sides and grenades were exploding on the LZ just behind us. Lane checked the team and then moved us quickly uphill, away from the fire. We were moving at a pretty fast clip for a recon team, but the quick movement broke us free from the enemy's ambush. Had the enemy opened fire just seconds earlier, we would have been caught in a cross fire in the open LZ. The enemy was attempting to follow and, all of a sudden, the bark on the tree next to me exploded as a burst of AK-47 rounds hit it. I crouched down and turned around to see a number of uniformed NVA regulars crossing the LZ, in hot pursuit on our back trail. I armed the LAW and fired it into their midst. This definitely put the "fear of God" into those who survived the explosion; and I was then able to turn and run to catch the team.

Lane had called the choppers for extraction and they were on the way back to us as we continued up the hill. The enemy force had been stopped momentarily by the LAW that I had fired on them. This brief delay in their pursuit allowed the team to put some distance between us and our enemy. We crossed over a ridge line and into a small valley on the other side. The triple canopy of the jungle made it quite difficult for a helicopter extraction; however, the nature of the undergrowth gave us some cover from the enemy. Lane had the Vietnamese members of the team backtrack to the top of the ridge and plant M-14 mines (toe poppers) in our back trail, while he and I set up a few claymores facing in that general direction. We had found a small break in the upper canopy and would ask for the choppers to drop McGuire Rigs for our extraction.

The Marines had made it back before the Slicks and were busy strafing the LZ and hillsides with mini guns and rocket fire. When the Slicks arrived, we marked our position with pen flares, shot straight up through the opening. We all felt great relief as that beautiful helicopter hovered overhead and dropped the McGuire rigs down to us.

Lane signaled for me to go first, so I sat on the nylon strap and arranged my right hand in the hand loop. Ha and Sau got on the other rigs and Lane signaled the crew chief to take us up. As the chopper lifted, it moved forward and dragged us through the branches of the treetops. My rucksack was ripped from my shoulders and I almost lost my CAR 15. Ha and Sau were scratched up a bit, but otherwise in one piece, still seated in their rigs.

As we cleared the treetops, we could see the distinctive explosion of white phosphorus near the LZ. We watched in awe, as a pair of "fast movers" (F4 Phantom Jets) dove down toward the white phosphorus and dropped canisters of napalm, which exploded splashing liquid flames over the LZ and the hillside. The heat was so intense that I am surprised that we were not burned hanging there, 100-ft below our helicopter and perhaps 150-feet over the flames.

As we flew off to the east, we saw the second Slick hovering over Lane, Owen and Hiep and watched as the three cleared the treetops. We flew the 50-miles back to FOB 1, dangling 100-feet below the helicopters, and were lowered down slowly on the airstrip at Phu Bai, happy to be alive and whole.

This was the only mission that I would run with Bob Owen and the last with Glen Lane and ST Idaho. The next day I was reassigned upon recommendation of Lane, as One Zero of ST New Jersey. Three months later, on May 23, 1968, Lane and Owen were lost with four other Idaho warriors on a mission in Laos. They remain listed as Missing in Action to this day. Had Lane not recommended me for ST New Jersey, I would have most likely been with ST Idaho on that fateful day.

SFC Glenn O Lane, MIA 23 May 1968

Purple Heart

Bronze Star

FOB 1 Short Rounds

"Thou shall not steal"

The SOG mission in Southeast Asia was to run long range probes behind enemy lines. The military allocated equipment based on the operational assignment of the units. Since our mission was classified Top Secret and involved long range missions launched by plane or helicopter, we were not allocated much in the way of ground transportation. We had a few deuce and a halves, an ambulance, a three quarter ton Jeep pickup, a five ton water truck, and one Jeep allotted for the FOB. At times, this left us with no ground transportation to the range, the Marine base, or to the city of Hue.

One morning at formation, the First Sergeant told us that we could really use a few more Jeeps if anyone happened to find an "unwanted" one. Later that day, I had accompanied my friend Ken Cryan on the "water run" to the Marine Base. The "water run" was a daily chore at the camp, since there was no running water and local sources of water were highly contaminated with unwanted minerals, fecal matter and a host of human parasites. To keep the troops healthy, the - ton water truck was driven to the First Marine Division headquarters each day and filled with purified water from the line of truck mounted ERDalators (truck mounted water purification, micro filtering system). These systems removed about 99.9% of harmful substances from the brackish water of streams or rice paddies. The purified water was used for drinking, cooking, washing, and showering at FOB 1.

After the tanker was full, we drove the short distance through the Marine base to the Post Exchange (PX). The PX was a fairly good size for being located in a combat zone. I would estimate its size at about 40,000 square feet, containing everything from greeting cards to send home, to cameras, civilian clothing and engagement rings. On this day, we stopped for cigarettes and toothpaste.

On our way out, we spotted a brand new, shiny Jeep in perfect condition. The OD (Army green, olive drab) paint shined as though it had been waxed, the seats had some sort of fancy seat covers, and there was a big brass dice for a gearshift knob. Ken and I decided that this would make the perfect addition to our collection back at FOB 1. Of course, it would need to be remodeled to suite our more clandestine needs. I got in and started the Jeep with my fingernail clippers and took off for the safety of FOB 1. Once I went through the locked gate, there was little chance that the Jeep, as it now appeared, would ever be seen again by its prior owner.

I drove the Jeep directly to the motor pool and told the Vietnamese workers there to age the Jeep a little with a few dents, dropping and cracking the windshield, and painting it black to match the rest of our fleet. The seat covers were trashed and the fancy gear shift knob was thrown into the old, French minefield surrounding the camp. The Vietnamese worked fast and within an hour, the new Jeep was transformed into an old, beat up, black Jeep. When their work was complete, the Jeep was parked amidst our other vehicles in the hot sun.

About two hours after returning with the prize, I was helping Ken pump the water into the large tank over the camps makeshift shower, when we noticed an unfamiliar army colonel and his escort entering the CO's office (since FOB 1 was a TOP Secret facility, only assigned personnel or those "passed" in by camp security could enter). After a few minutes, he returned to the street, accompanied by our CO and the First Sergeant. They were headed toward the back of the camp, where the motor pool and the vehicles were located. When we emptied the water truck, we drove it back to its parking place and observed the officers standing near the freshly, stolen Jeep talking to one another. We parked our truck and went about our business.

Later that afternoon, all the American personnel were called to a special formation. This was out of the ordinary, since normally only one morning formation was called each day. While all hands stood at attention, the Commanding Officer told us of his "Visit" from the Commanding Officer of the CID (Criminal Investigative Division). He said that the Colonel was duly impressed by our stealth, our ability to steal his Jeep, and then to make it disappear. Ken and I stood there, not knowing whether to be afraid of pending doom or proud of our accomplishment. The CO then announced that he wanted those responsible to report to his office immediately following the formation. After a few more announcements, we were dismissed.

Ken and I briefly discussed our options and then reported to the CO's office. We admitted that we had stolen the Jeep and brought it to FOB 1 for SOG use. The CO then told us that we were not too smart to bring home that particular Jeep. However, the CID officer was so impressed that we got away with it, that he was going to just order himself another Jeep. The CO then asked us where we had stashed the Jeep and we told him that it was parked in plain sight near the motor pool. The CO then had us walk him out there and show him the Jeep. Our commander laughed when he saw it, and noted that they had stood nearby and that the "remodeling job" was such that the CID commander had not recognized "his" Jeep. He then shared that the Colonel had been so impressed with our prowess, as well as our need for vehicles, that he had promised to direct any recovered vehicles for our use.

Andy the Pig

Colonel Snell had been given a piglet by a local province chief as a sign of friendship. A pen was constructed close the trench line, near the back of the camp where the pig was fed all the table scraps and leftovers from the mess hall. The pig was named Andy, after a Master Sergeant who was in charge of the Green Beret Lounge at FOB 1. The pig grew quite large over time and became sort of a pet to some of us in the camp.

After too many beers we would often leave heavy set and pig-like Andy, the club manager, behind his bar in the club and wander out to visit Andy, the pig. On occasion, a red checkered tablecloth was brought along and one of my adventurous friends would climb into Andy's pen for a friendly "pig fight." This was a crazy show of the astonished pig running around the pen squealing, trying his best to stay away from the drunk and fearless "matador." Andy and the occasional pig fights were good distractions from the dangerous missions and the daily life away from home.

The men of SOG fought hard, and many died hard, so it was perfectly acceptable for us to also play hard. When we were not on a mission or out training for one, it was quite normal to consume huge amounts of beer and other adult beverages. To make life simple, little ticket books (called chits) were sold and used as the only currency in the Green Beret Lounge. Each chit was worth twenty five cents and could be exchanged for one beer or mixed drink. It was, therefore, very cheap to get quite pleasantly drunk on our down time.

Green Beret Lounge (the club), FOB 1

The Green Beret Lounge was a place for social interaction within FOB 1. It was one of the few air-conditioned places in the compound and therefore, a good place to escape the almost unbearable heat and humidity of Southeast Asia. The "Clubs" jukebox often blared out country and western tunes favored by the older NCOs (30-40), while most of the young guys (20-30) would listen to the sounds of the sixties in their hootches while sharing the latest cannabis with a few close friends.

The different tastes in music broke the camp down into several cultural classes, not too different from what was happening back home. The sounds of Jimmy Hendrix, Janice Joplin, or Bob Dylan rang out from the sophisticated contemporary sound systems in the hootches, while the shit-kicker sounds of Texas and Oklahoma reigned in the Club. The young guys (the heads) and the old guys (the shit kickers) had to trust each other with their very lives and respected each other more than brothers. The walls of the generation or cultural gap fell within the smoky confines of the Green Beret Lounge.

We would gather there as a family to share a drink, a sad story of a lost friend, or the joy of something good happening back in the world. We, the young warriors of SOG, would tolerate that shit-kicker music of the old guys, while we shared with our brothers at arms.

Late one afternoon, I was sitting alone at the bar, having a refreshing beer and chatting with the club manager's Vietnamese girlfriend. The club was almost empty and quiet that afternoon, but would soon fill as the evening wore on. As I sat savoring the last of my beer, an older guy in jungle fatigues asked if he could join me. I did not recognize him nor bother to look too closely at his uniform in the dim light of the club. He asked if he could buy me a beer and I responded, telling him only if I could buy him one. We laughed and introduced ourselves to each other. I just about choked on my beer and fell off my stool trying to clamber to my feet when the "man" introduced himself as William Westmoreland. As I caught my breath and stood in amazement, the powerful General William C. Westmoreland just laughed and told me to sit and enjoy my beer. This was the most powerful military man in Vietnam, the commanding officer of all US forces in Southeast Asia, and he was sitting at a bar, having a beer with me.

He told me that he was in I Corps (northernmost military section of South Vietnam) for a meeting and just wanted a few minutes of quiet time. He asked about my family back home and about my assignment in SOG. He was a really nice guy and I really enjoyed meeting and talking to this great man. Some of the "shit kickers" came in during our visit and when they saw who I was sitting with; they sort of sheepishly slithered over to a corner table, near the juke box and kept to themselves. I'll never forget my good friend and One Zero SFC Glenn Lane busting my ass later that evening, about drinking with the General.

An old tradition in SOG found its way to FOB 1 and the Green Beret Lounge. Just to keep things friendly and not too serious, someone would occasionally walk in the door of the club and shout "anybody who can't tap dance is queer." It was a real sight to see every man in the club jump to their feet and start tap dancing to beat the band. The later in the evening it got, the more energetically these warriors would dance. I have been a happy tap dancer in various bars in Vietnam and in airports, clubs, and meetings in the United States. This crazy tradition continues to this day, where men of SOG gather together.

Andy's Demise

There came a happy and a sad day to FOB 1 in 1968. A number of the "shit kickers" were going home (alive) and a big celebration was being planned. Our friend Andy the pig was leaving with them, but not on a big assed bird like the others. I took a truck to Hue and purchased a number of 100 pound blocks of ice. The ice was frozen in an ice plant in the old city, and the 100 pound blocks would be used to ice down the drinks for the party.

Before getting the ice, I had flown to the airfield in Da Nang and traded an enemy AK-47, complete with enemy blood stains, for a whole pallet of Crown Royal. The Crown Royal was loaded on a "blackbird" and flown to the Marine Airfield at Phu Bai. From there, it was loaded on a deuce and a half and hauled to FOB 1. The traditional Crown Royal fifths were removed from their royal purple, velvet bags and iced down in a ¾ ton Jeep trailer. The ice was first broken up; using sledge hammers and the finished product was a big heap of icy chunks littered with the fancy Crown Royal bottles. The trailer was positioned in front of the club and there were plenty of bottles for everyone.

Before the drinking began, a very special dinner was being served in the US mess hall that afternoon. A few special friends from the Marine base had been invited to join the festivities that day and so the "family" was expanded for this big sendoff celebration. As we entered the mess hall that day, there was a long buffet table set with lines of hungry warriors, splitting on either side of the table. The first thing we saw as we approached the table was the roasted head of our friend Andy the pig. A shit-kicker had donated his boonies hat for Andy to wear and a big cigar, like those smoked by Andy, the club manager, was smoldering away in Andy the pig's mouth. The allure of all of the wonderful food on the table was thwarted for some by this shocking appearance of our friend, Andy. I remember a few (won't mention any names) who, with tears in their eyes, ate salad that day or simply left the mess hall and returned to the festivities later that day. I enjoyed the meal and when I was leaving, I noticed that someone had exchanged that nasty, old cigar with a joint. Poor Andy had gone out in style for sure and there were pig fights nevermore.

After the meal, the party was on and Crown Royal was enjoyed by all. The bottles were retrieved from the ice, opened and drank like individual beers. Needless to say, there was not a sober breath taken that night at FOB 1. Later on that night, word went out secretly among the "heads" that an after party would be held on top of the new command bunker at 2300 hrs. It was ok to get drunk on Crown Royal, so the collective shit-kicker, heads party was held in the wide open spaces of the camp. The after party was for those to share memories with trusted friends over a bowl or two. None of the heads knew for certain who did or did not partake in the cannabis and so the message of the after party was shared from mouth to mouth, to those who, in fact, were known.

At 2300 hrs, a whole lot of quite drunk warriors found their way to the roof of the new command bunker to pass a bowl around in honor of our departing brothers. Each of us was as astonished as the next that the attendees included most of the US personnel from the camp, including "shit kickers" and even officers. The party ended and the following day, we all paid hell with horrific hangovers for what we had consumed. Life returned to normal in the camp, with small social groups meeting here and there to share their various music and other choices. The club remained the center of social life at FOB 1 and we all missed our departed friends, including Andy, the pig.

The Tank

One sunny afternoon, during the late monsoons of 1968, one of our indigenous personnel, Khanh Van Doan (Cowboy) was returning from visiting friends in the village of Phu Luong with five other indigenous SOG personnel. Three of the men were in their uniforms and the other three were dressed in

Patton M48 tank

civilian clothing. As they were walking the short distance, along South Vietnam Highway One, from the village to FOB 1, they came upon a US Marine Corp tank crew and their broken down tank. It seems that the tank had lost a tread and was crippled on the side of the road, on the hillside, below the camp. The tank was an M48 Patton tank and fully capable of unleashing a whole lot of whoop ass.

Unfortunately, one of the bedraggled tank crew and our Cowboy had a bit of an altercation. It seemed that the Marines had visited a whorehouse in the village and had been robbed by some local gangsters. They had accused our SOG team members in civilian clothing of being those gangsters. The Marine starting getting rough with the accused and Cowboy and the other two uniformed SOG team members attempted to tell the Marines that the men were not gangsters, but SOG employees out of uniform. The Marine refused to believe Cowboys' story and continued harassing the three men. Cowboy and the other two uniformed men beat feet back to the FOB for help. It was common for US forces to be disrespectful to the smaller Vietnamese or Nungs (descendants of Chinese ancestors) that they would encounter in country. To most US soldiers "they" were all the same: North Vietnamese, VC, Chinese, and the young Americans serviceman had no reason for getting to know the indigenous populations. The men of Special Forces and SOG, on the other hand, formed tight bonds of friendship and camaraderie that exist to this day with their indigenous counterparts. After all, we held each other's lives in our hands each time we embarked on a mission, and so, we were, a "band of brothers."

left to right: Steve Perry, Cowboy, Robert Shippen, Bruce Johnston

The poor, America Marine tanker had chosen poorly that day deciding to push around our friends and team members. When Cowboy returned to FOB 1 and told us what had happened, the word spread quickly through te recon community. About twenty of us donned our web gear, grabbed our weapons, and loaded on a truck. With me on that truck were Sgt Tim Kirk and Specialist 5 Ken Cryan, along with twenty Vietnamese (there may have been others on that day and they are not intentionally omitted). It truly must have been a terrifying site for that tank crew to see twenty or so heavily armed, unconventional looking warriors jump off that old, black truck and surround their tank. Cowboy pointed out the culprit and as our band of brothers locked and loaded their CAR 15s, pointing them menacingly at the tank crew, I had the honor of "instructing" the offender. As the would be "tough guy" GI got a little huffy, my team member and friend, Tim Kirk locked and loaded a round in the chamber of his CAR 15, pointing it menacingly at him. Believe it or not, the young man settled right down and listened to what we had to say.

As we stood there talking to the young man, I saw someone poke their head out of the tanks turret, and reach for the machine gun mounted there. Quick as lightening, one of the Vietnamese climbed aboard, behind the turret, and put the muzzle of his CAR 15 to the back of the head, of the would be machine gunner. I told the young offender about the reasons for US involvement in Southeast Asia which he had apparently forgotten, about our special relationship with the Vietnamese people, and that to harm one of them was to harm one of us. He promised "never, never, never" to bother another friendly Vietnamese, and I promised that we would return if he did.

After that, we loaded up and drove back to the camp. Later, we stood at the trench line, watching the tank turn its turret toward the camp, wondering if we had incited more trouble than we needed for the day. The tank crew eventually got their tank under way and rumbled off into the distance. It was a relief to see them go, but we will always wonder what kind of crazy tale they would tell about the incident. The day ended with Cowboy's ego bruised, but our bonds of friendship and trust, stronger than ever. In fact, we get together each year at our annual Special Operations Association reunions in Las Vegas and often retelling the story with old friends.

The Big Bang

When we weren't either training for a mission or on one, we would all pitch in to help with the tasks of keeping the camp up and running. On one such day, I was assisting my roommate and best friend in Vietnam, SP5 Ken Cryan, with the production and installation of a few new urinals for the Cambodians, housed toward the front of the camp. These were to consist of 55 gallon drums, buried flush with ground level, open on the top, and filled with crushed stone. The urine would leach out into the surrounding clay soils through holes in the bottom of the drum.

We went to the Marine Airfield and gathered up a number of empty 55-gallon drums and brought them to the back of the camp. We placed the barrels in an area which was surrounded on three sides by sand bag walls. The open side of the area faced the rice paddies in the distance. In order to make the urinals, we had to cut the tops off the 55 gallon, steel drums. Since we had neither giant can opener nor an acetylene cutting torch, we chose to use explosives to cut the tops off the drums.

Neither Ken nor I were "real" experts with explosives, but we both loved blowing things up and figured we knew enough to get the job done. There were enough explosives in the FOB ammo dump to blow up just about anything you could imagine. There were pallets full of C-4 plastic explosive in 2.5 pound blocks, many rolls of DET. Cord, along with a plethora of mines, rockets, grenades, and small arms ammunition.

Ken and I choose DET. cord as our tool of choice for opening these 55-gallon "cans." DET. Cord is a flexible tube filled with a white explosive called PETN. The cord looks like that white plastic coated clothesline rope but is much more deadly. The PETN DET. Cord burns (read explodes) at an incredible rate of 26,000 feet per second. This means that if you light off one end, the resultant "fire" will reach nearly 5 miles distance (4.92 miles) in just one second. The cord is "ignited" with a blasting cap and a timed fuse to allow the operator time to escape.

One time around the topside lip of the drum with the DET. Cord and we decided that it would probably be better if we packed the cord with something to direct the blast down toward the steel that we were trying to cut. The clay soil was our first choice, but we found it too dry and crumbly at the time. Next choice for the "packing" was the silly-putty like C4. C4 or Composition 4 is explosives mixed in with plastic, putty like binders. The material burns even faster than DET. Cord at an incredible, 18,000 miles per hour. The malleable and somewhat sticky nature of the C4 made it work well to pack the DET. cord and help hold it in place. We probably used about three pounds of C4 between the two barrels. We applied a ten second fuse to the end of the DET. Cord, took a close look to ensure that no one was in the immediate or surrounding blast area, and posted a guard at the path leading to the occupied end of the camp. The fuse was ignited, and Ken and I took cover in the trench line.

When the blast occurred, chunks of the 55 gallon drums, no larger than a man's fist, flew for hundreds of yards in every direction. The only thing that remained of the drum job was the widely scattered scraps and a scorched crater at ground zero. The intensity of the blast had led the ARVN (Army of the Republic of Viet Nam) compound next door and the Marine artillery up the road to believe that we were under attack. Their 155mm guns began sending out defensive fire to our North and East Perimeters, while everyone at FOB 1 poured out into the bunkers and trenches that surrounded the camp. It was quite a show for about thirty minutes before the "all clear" was sent around and the cease fire order was issued. Once again, Ken and I had a lot of explaining to do before the sun set that evening over the Green Beret Lounge.

I don't remember if those urinals were ever finished or not but will always remember and cherish this experience that I shared with my friend, Ken Cryan.

MACE

Mace was first developed in 1962 and consisted of an aerosol preparation of 1% CN gas (tear gas) in a solvent base. Today, the substance is unlawful in most countries because of its toxicity. It has been replaced with pepper spray, which is a preparation or Capsaicin, a mucous membrane irritating substance found in hot chili peppers which is less toxic than CN gas and is available for personal defense purposes in most of the United States.

MACV SOG was always on the cutting edge of developing weaponry. At some point in 1968, the supply sergeant told me he had received a shipment of a substance that could facilitate the capture of enemy prisoners. Since capturing of prisoners was always part of a recon team's mission, I picked up a few cans and brought them back to the hooch. One evening Ken Cryan, Ron Romancik and a few other friends were sitting around the hooch after a few drinks in the club and discussing the curious OD green aerosol cans sitting on my window sill. I explained that they were designed to temporarily blind and incapacitate an enemy, so that he could be cuffed and taken prisoner.

Ken, who was a sturdy, muscular, football player-type, young man from San Mateo California, scoffed at the idea and said that he did not believe that the stuff would work. After a few more drinks, and to the timeless sounds of Bob Dylan's "Masters of War," booming from the Teac™ reel to real tape recorder, a challenge went out from Ken.

My fearless and mellow friend, Ken Cryan, said that he would stand at one side of the hooch, with me on the other side, and bet me a drink that I could not hit him with the MACE and that if I did, in fact hit him that it would not incapacitate him.

As the song ended, we took our places across from each other, with our friends as witnesses to the event. We stood as if in a duel, as I raised the can and pulled the trigger. A stream of liquid crossed the room in an instant, hitting Ken right between the eyes. Ken grabbed for his normally ruddy face, which had immediately turned bright red and he gasped in pain. His eyes were forced closed by extreme burning and his nose began running and drool dropped from his lips. We gathered up our friend and took him next door to the dispensary, where we rinsed his face and eyes thoroughly with fresh clean water. Ken remained incapacitated for about an hour. When he finally recovered, he said "you win, what do you want to drink?" We all laughed and continued our camaraderie with a new respect for MACE.

Our friend Ken died in a lonely place in Laos, about a month after the MACE incident and I shall always remember his smile and mellow spirit. His death and the shenanigans of our politicians back in Washington at the time always bring me back to Dylan's lyrics from "Masters of War." Ken's sacrifice and those of over 50,000 brave Americans were thrown away by lesser men working on their political careers at the Paris Peace accords.

Many of my friends and brothers have died because of the inability of our politicians to take care of business back home. Their jobs and their public opinion polls were too important, their honor and commitment to the people of South Vietnam and to American sons did not match the honor and commitment of the young men they sent to do their dirty work. May God have mercy on their souls.

God Forbid that we should make the same mistake in Iraq and Afghanistan. If we start a fight, then we should finish it; and if we make a promise, we should keep it!

Catholic nuns and priests hitching a ride in a FOB 1 3/4 ton truck

Hue City shopping 1968

Rats, Rats, BIG Rats

During the Monsoon rains of 1968, three Vietnamese adults from the village of Phu Bai came to the dispensary, seeking our diagnosis and treatment. Hearing their disease symptoms brought our thoughts back to our days in Special Forces Medical Training at Ft. Bragg, North Carolina. They presented with fevers of 104-105F, chills, white coatings on their tongues, nausea, vomiting, body aches, and large swollen lymph nodes in their groins and thighs. They reported that the first symptoms appeared only a few days earlier, and that they were neighbors in the village.

Chills and high fevers were seen commonly in the local population who had malaria, but the lymph nodes, coated tongues, and close proximity of living quarters brought back what we had learned in a tropical disease class back at Fort Bragg, North Carolina. Our trainers had gone into the origins of diseases, how they are spread, the life cycles of pathogens, etc. With regard to the Plague of Europe during the Dark Ages, we had learned that it had killed more people than any other disease known to man. Nearly 200,000,000 worldwide had died of the dreaded "Black Death." A pandemic around 1328, it spread through Europe like a wildfire, killing off about one of every three humans. The symptoms of the three villagers and later lab results confirmed that they had Bubonic Plague.

As a child, you probably remember chanting a rhyme that went something like this:

> Ring around the rosies,
> a pocket full of posies,
> Ashes, ashes!
> We all fall down.

What the rhyme meant:

Ring around the rosies,
  (The rosary beads used to pray for the sick and dying)
A pocket full of posies,
  (Flowers carried in the pocket to cover the stench or the dead and dying)
Ashes, ashes!
  (Ashes everywhere from the burning bodies in the streets in an attempt to stop the spread or the disease)
We all fall down.
  (Everyone is dying)

Wow! The shock of the Black Death has been carried across the centuries and cultures to this very day, in a children's nursery rhyme. I am sure that you can imagine the shock of the American personnel in FOB 1 to hear that the safe haven of our base camp could fall to the unseen enemy that had killed off a third of Europe. All American's had received plague vaccines before leaving the US; however, we knew that they were only effective for about six months. Furthermore, the majority of the fighting men in the camp were Cambodians, Vietnamese, and Nungs who had not been vaccinated and were serving on the Hatchet Force and the Recon teams. We had to act, and act quickly, to prevent the spread of the disease to the camp.

Our training came into play once again. The plague is spread to humans by lice and fleas that live their lives parasitically on rats from the genus *Rattus* and species *rattus* or *norvegicus* . *Rattus Norvegicus* is the brown rat, which originally came from Egypt (remember the 10 plagues of Egypt described in the biblical chapter of Exodus), but are now found worldwide, common in populated areas. They can be found in the sewers of New York City, the sugarcane fields of Hawaii, and the rice paddies and villages of Southeast Asia.

Rats feed at night and we had seen them many times scurrying around the mess hall and the trenches within FOB 1. Rats forage great distances for food, returning to the same areas night after night, where they have had success. In those areas, they establish colonies which continue to grow until the food is exhausted. The concern was that the infected rats in the village would spread the disease to the rat population that journeyed each night through the rice paddies and mine fields, back to the camp. Once diseased rats were inside the camp, it would not be long before the disease would spread quickly through the human population.

A meeting was called with Colonel Snell, the Commanding Officer. The Colonel listened to our concerns and assigned my friend and fellow medic Ron Romancik, to immediately undertake a program to rid the camp of existing rats and thus reduce or eliminate the threat of disease. Rats would often be seen feeding on scraps of food dropped by the indigenous personnel in the defensive trenches that surrounded the camp. Ron was one of my favorite people in the camp and we spent a lot of time together when not on a mission. We shared many a good laugh between the tears shed for our fallen brothers. Ron was enthusiastic about his new assignment, which he named "The Rat Patrol." After the meeting with the Colonel, we retired to the Green Beret Lounge for a few beers and to discuss how Ron wanted to attack the rats.

As we sat smoking and drinking in the dimly lit bar, I told Ron and the others about one of the sick, twisted members of my SF Medic's class. When we were taught about *Rattus rattus*, we all thought that the name was quite funny, but, after hearing how fast rats reproduce, a classmate invented a far superior rat. He drew out a cartoon character of a tall, skinny, overly endowed rat standing on its hind legs and named it Biggus rattus. And so, a new species was born that day who had become our class mascot and whose image was reproduced from North Carolina to Germany, to Panama and to Vietnam, as my classmates were assigned to the various Special Forces Groups around the world. We all had a good laugh over Biggus as we planned our attack on his descendants.

Ron had many ingenious ideas on how to control the rat population, which led to many hilarious adventures and a bunch of dead rats. The first assault began that very night as those who volunteered for rat duty went to the armory and checked out Sten Guns, Swedish Ks, and 22 caliber pistols with silencers. The plan was this, after the Cambodians ("Bodes") had completed their evening meal (many ate in the trenches on the camps perimeter because it was cooler than their mess hall), and after dark, the "Rat Patrol" would hunt the perimeter with the silenced weapons and shoot the rats feeding on what the "Bodes" had dropped.

The Trenchline

The first assault was considered a great success and a lot of fun by the "Rat Patrol." During the debriefing at the Green Beret Lounge, concerns about human safety were raised. The trenches zig-zagged around the camp perimeter connected mortar pits and bunkers provided protection as we would defend. The many zigs and zags would prevent shrapnel or small arms fire from traveling very far down the trench. Every night, guards were positioned at strategic points around the perimeter to watch for enemy movement outside the mine field. Other men would commonly go to the trenches to visit a friend on guard duty, to have a smoke, or just to look over the rice paddies and the village beyond. Since the rat hunt was being conducted with silenced, fully automatic weapons in the dark, it could be possible for an unaware man to wander around a corner in the trench or exit a bunker just as a burst of gunfire was fired at a rat. We all agreed that Ron would have to come up with a new plan of attack; and he did just that on the following day. The following morning, several of us donned surgical gloves and masks and walked the trenches to retrieve the bodies of the dead rats. About a dozen bodies were retrieved and put in plastic bags and removed from the camp.

Later that day, we went to the village with an interpreter from the camp and a 20-pound bag of rat poison-infused grain. By talking to the locals, we were directed to the huts where our Plague patients lived. Although Phu Luong was only a few kilometers south of the "big city" of Hue, it was a rural farming village and very rustic. The village was bisected by the North South "Highway" 1 and there were one or two unpaved side streets. The majority of the village was connected by walking paths between rustic shacks and huts.

Kids in Phu Luong, Ron Romancik photo

There were no doors or windows on most of the buildings, allowing chickens and pigs to wander where they may. The simple peasants who lived here had never known the luxury of trash cans, so the trash and garbage from each dwelling was simply stacked outside the door opening until it could be carted out of the village in a basket. The trash piles were an open invitation to the hungry rats that had colonized the village shortly after the humans started living there. The domestic chickens and pigs also foraged for food and looked for treats in the trash piles. As we observed the chickens pecking around the trash, we realized that our plan to sprinkle the poison around had to be modified. A search of the area revealed several rat holes. Poison grain was dumped into each and then the holes were covered with heavy rocks to prevent access by children or chickens. We also tried the rat poison back at the camp, but found that the rats would eat all the poison and come back for more. We needed something faster if we were to rid the camp of the rats and prevent an outbreak of Plague.

Ron Romancik had already decided on the faster, cleaner way to go. He would go to Hue and buy a cobra. He would release the cobra into the rat holes and the cobra would eat all the rats. The cobra was purchased and released with little effect other than pissing off the CO who was quite phobic about snakes, the CO referred to the cobra as "Jake No Shoulders." I remember the CO yelling at Ron and saying that he "better get Jake out of that rat hole." All this excitement, but Ron, in his unruffled response, had both an explanation for why project cobra had "failed" and how he planned to get "Jake No Shoulders." He deduced that the cobra would kill a rat, eat it, and then sleep a week or so until he was hungry enough to find another rat. His plan to get "Jake" was to have a mongoose flown in from Okinawa and send him down the rat hole. After some thought and a few more visits to the Green Beret Lounge, it was decided that the biological cure of the mongoose was going to take too long and a more expedient plan was devised.

I shared how I had been raised in Whittier, California on a residential lot, bordered on one side by a large commercial orange grove. My parents had beautiful flowers, vegetables and fruit trees in the back yard; and an army of gophers from the orange grove would burrow under the fence and dine on the roots of our garden. My father's solution was an effective and simple one. A garden hose was plugged into the exhaust pipe of the family automobile, stuck down the gopher hole and after running the car's engine for awhile, the carbon monoxide in the exhaust would kill the gophers. It was decided to give carbon monoxide a try for both "Jake" and the rats. We plugged a length of tubing into the rat hole that "Jake" had crawled into. The other end of the hose was plugged into the exhaust pipe of a Jeep with the engine running for about an hour, and until fumes were detected coming from other rat holes under the same building.

With victory in sight, we returned to the dispensary to plan our next move. A short while later, camp engineer Kenneth Cryan stopped by to tell us that he had seen a large snake crawling into a rat hole under the building where the Commanding Officer had his office. Ron Romancik's pale, Polish complexion turned a "whiter shade of pale" as he considered the horror of the CO finding out that "Jake" had taken up residence under his office. The CO's ophidiophobia may likely lead to some harsh reaction on his part; and so, the Rat Patrol needed a swift and sure means of ridding the camp of the deadly cobra. Ken had the perfect, fast, and effective plan. The camps ammo dump had an ample supply of munitions and explosives of all types. The new battle plan was to thread Det cord into the rat hole as far as it would go and then to detonate it to kill "Jake."

Ken brought up a roll of Det cord and Ron began feeding it into the rat hole until it hit something. The cord was cut from the roll and a detonator with a four second fuse was attached. The perimeter of the building was checked to make sure that everyone was clear and the pin was pulled on the detonator. The resulting explosion brought most of the camp running, with weapons in hand, as if we were under attack.

Among those arriving at the scene was the CO himself. If you had never seen a black army officer turn red in the face, this was the place to see it. The Colonel was really pissed and the Rat Patrol feared the worst. Ron, Ken, and I were "invited" to visit the CO in the privacy of his office. As we walked in, we gasped at what we saw. An area of the Commanders concrete floor was all broken up and concrete dust had settled everywhere. The CO demanded an explanation for the explosion and destruction of his office floor. Ron nervously explained the story as the CO dusted off his chair and took a seat. The CO turned to the camp engineer and asked how he did not predict the destruction of his floor, while utilizing high explosives in the rat hole. Ken explained that the concrete slabs were four inches thick and should not have been damaged, since most of the blast would be directed out the rat hole as in a cannon shot. Ken picked up a big chunk of the floor and showed it to the colonel, explaining that the damaged area only appeared to be about two inches thick. It also appeared, from the intensity of the blast in the damaged area that the DET cord had coiled up in a rats nest, thus intensifying the blast in that area.

The CO said that he would think about what to do with us and ordered us to clean up the loose concrete and repair it. We went to supply, got a few tools and a wheelbarrow and returned to the office. As we removed the loose chunks of concrete under the watchful eye of the Colonel, we uncovered the bodies of two rats, in what appeared to be their nest, and a few minutes later, to everyone's astonishment, the very dead body of "Jake" was uncovered. The dead were carefully removed, put in the wheelbarrow and buried at the back of the camp.

When we returned, several Vietnamese workmen were repairing the concrete and the CO was there waiting for us. It seemed that he was so pleased with our successful mission against the cobra and the rats that he wanted to reward us with a beer at the Green Beret Lounge. During this brief visit with the CO, he suggested that Ron find a less explosive means to kill off the remaining rats.

One option that had not been yet used on the rats was fire. A plan was formulated to deliver JP-4 (jet fuel) down the rat holes and then to ignite the vaporized accelerant. This, Ron believed, would send the rats fleeing to the rice paddies. The delivery systems were the three-gallon insecticide hand pump sprayers that were used for mosquito control.

The monsoon season was fully upon us, and all missions were on a weather hold. This was a memorable time for me. The camp was like home away from home. The men of SOG were my extended family, with whom I ate, drank, worked, and played. The Rat Patrol had become a challenge, shared by close brothers, in a far away land. We spent much of our time on those rainy, monsoon days plotting and planning our next move against *Rattus*.

The jet fuel was loaded and the attack was launched on one of the rainiest days I had ever experienced. The ground had standing water everywhere. The cans were pumped up and sprayed into the rat holes under the concrete slabs.

A match was thrown in the hole and a whooshing sound would be followed by a blue flame, shooting out of the hole like the back of a jet engine. About a dozen of these holes were fired with nothing unusual happening, other than the warriors getting soaked by the rain.

It was assumed that since the rats are nocturnal, that they were sleeping and had probably been consumed by the flames or been asphyxiated when the oxygen was all used up in the rat holes. On the next firing, a burning rat came barreling out of the flames, headed for the camps perimeter and the rice paddies beyond. It was a rather funny sight as the rat ran through puddles about one inch deep looking like a small jet ski leaving a wake and a smoke trail. The body of this hairless, charred rat was later recovered in the trenches.

On a subsequent hole under the Cambodian mess hall, a burning rat ran out of the hole, saw us, turned and scurried behind the corrugated metal siding of the building. A short while later, we pitched in on a bucket brigade to extinguish the fire in order to save what remained of the mess hall.

The Rat Patrol had completed its mission and was soon disbanded. We had a diminished rat population and no more cases of Bubonic Plague to treat. Shortly after this mission was completed, Ken Cryan volunteered for a position on an ST. He was assigned as the One One on ST Alabama, under the command of One Zero, John Allen.

On 4 May 1968, Ken Cryan was killed while being extracted from a target in Laos beyond the northern ridges of the Ashau Valley. The murderous bastards had shot Ken and a Nung team member about thirty times while they were wounded and helpless hanging on a jungle penetrator being used to extract them. On this mission, the entire team was killed except SSGT John Allen, who managed to escape by running/falling down a steep hillside, thus evading the enemy.

Special Forces medic PFC Paul King, and the remaining Nung members of the team were killed on the ground, their bodies were never to be recovered. I had ST New Jersey on a mission close by and listened to the radio communications between PFC King and Covey. Covey reported to SSG Allen that Cryan was in the hospital and doing fine. When I returned from my mission later that day, I was asked to go to the morgue in Da Nang, with Romancik, to identify Ken's body. The memory and the pain of that day remain very vivid haunting me still.

Ron continued his work as a SOG medic, both in the dispensary and flying chase when teams were inserted or extracted. He now lives a "quiet" life as a retired pharmacist in New York State. Ron is a hero to me, as are all of the other men of SOG.

Long live Ron, Long live Biggus Rattus!

Ron Romancik 1968

My Band of Brothers

"We few, we happy few, we band of brothers. For he today that sheds his blood with me shall be my brother;" William Shakespeare

During the monsoon season, Lt Colonel Robert Lopez, our new FOB 1 commander, was most anxious to get "his" teams into our area of operation. Several of the STs had been assigned targets and the One Zeros made almost daily VRs by either helicopter or O-2 Skymaster aircraft. The target area consisted of extremely rough mountainous terrain covered by triple canopy jungle. It was the One Zero's mission to select a suitable location for his team to be inserted, either by landing a helicopter or by having the team rappel in on ropes suspended from the chopper. The VRs during those days and weeks never provided a view of anything, but clouds.

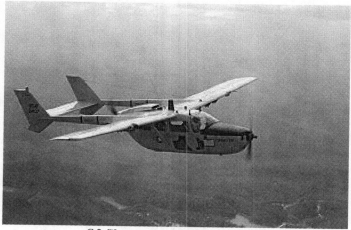

O2 Skymaster, Air Force photo

One day, while clouds still prohibited any teams from being inserted, the new commander called together some of the experienced team members, including Glenn Lane, John Allen and myself. He told us that he was under great pressure "from above" to get a team on the ground. He told us, "You guys are what the song is all about" referring to the Barry Sadler song "Ballad of the

Green Beret." He offered any team who would get on their target by walking the 50-miles or so though enemy infested terrain a week of rest and relaxation in Hawaii, complete with a thousand dollars in green money to spend. We all explained to the CO that such a walk would not be possible due to the terrain and the limitations on the small team's ability to carry enough supplies for such a long trek. We also explained that if the team ran into a fire fight, there was no way that air support could assist, or extract the team because of the weather. He insisted that it could be done and told us to think about his offer.

As we left the CO that day, we discussed what kind of stuff he must smoke in his pipe. We, who had flown to and inserted into the target area many times, could not believe that a sane man would suggest such a crazy plan.

CH 46 on FOB 1 airstrip photo courtesy of Ron Romancik

Several weeks after making his offer, the weather began to clear over the target area. Colonel Lopez learned of the development of a new (to him) type of jungle penetrator. This was a heavy, anchor-like device which could be dropped down through the jungle canopy on a winch cable from a hovering chopper. It would break branches along the way; and when it hit the ground, three seats would unfold. Three men from a SOG team could sit on it, strapping themselves to the device and be winched up to the safety of the helicopter. The device could also be used to insert a team by lowering the device with the team members aboard. This would allow a team to be inserted in areas where there was no clearing large enough for a landing zone (LZ).

We would end up riding the device out of the jungle on future missions. It would also be the place where my roommate would hang injured and defenseless, as his body was riddled by enemy bullets.

Colonel Lopez was so enthusiastic about this development that on 6 March 1968, he went along on a launch to observe an insertion procedure. He went over the objections of the Marine pilot, who explained that both the altitude and air temperature at the target would limit his ability to safely hover, and that the added weight of the CO could make it near impossible. The SOG commander rode along on the mission anyway.

The helicopter was a CH46A Chinook (Sea Knight) that had been modified specifically for the use of the Jungle penetrator. A hole had been cut in the floor, large enough for the penetrator and its cargo to pass through. A powerful winch was mounted overhead to lift the penetrator to safety. The mission failed as the chopper pilot attempted to hover over the target, losing his lift, which resulted in hitting the treetops with the choppers rotors. The failed insert was of a SOG six man recon team. The three Americans on the team were on TDY (temporary duty) from the 1st Special Forces group in Okinawa. The men were brand new in FOB 1 and I had never met any of them.

Fellow Special Forces Medic and friend Ron Romancik rode along in a second Chinook as the "chase medic." It was his job to observe the insertion as well as rescuing and or treating anyone injured during the insertion. This was a very dangerous job since the chase medic was by himself and would only be inserted after a gunfight or crash had already incapacitated other team members.

While Romancik hovered nearby in the chase chopper, the chopper with Colonel Lopez and the team from Okinawa crashed. The official government report says that the helicopter was shot down by enemy fire. However, Romancik and other later witnesses never observed any gunfire, or enemy contact at the site. Romancik requested to be lowered to the ground to assist an injured crew member that he observed in the clearing but the pilot of the chase helicopter did not allow Ron to go in and to assist the injured man or to look for other survivors. The jungle penetrator was lowered and the lone crewman was hoisted up. The chopper pulled away and delivered the wounded Marine to the hospital.

When Romancik returned to FOB 1, he learned that SOG medic Jerry Donley and ST member, Pat Johnson, had returned to the crash site to search for other survivors. Apparently Air Rescue was also on site and four additional crew members from the CH 46 were rescued.

The following day, a medic volunteer was sought to return to the crash site after SFC Skau saw mirror flashes nearby, while flying over the area in the COVEY plane. Ron Romancik volunteered for this dangerous one man Bright Light. Here is his story in his own words:

> "There I sat in the Kingbee watching the FOB disappearing from sight, no radio, no gunship, no one else. I said to myself, "this is your day to die." It didn't take long to get to the target. I was hoping it would have taken longer. The Kingbee flew around, checking the terrain and looking for a landing site. SFC Skau was above in Covey, giving him directions to the approximant location of the mirror flashes. I was in the chopper saying my prayers. Then the Kingbee started down.
>
> It got about fifty feet above the ground and started hovering. I could see a small clearing off the right side of the chopper that extended into a tree line. The only trouble was there was no place to land the chopper on the hillside. It was too steep for the Kingbee to set down. I looked over at the door gunner and he was hooking up a McGuire Rig to the rescue hoist. I said to myself "You are definitely going to die now." I got into the rig and he started to lower me down. While I was being lowered, there wasn't a shoot fired. The hill was steep. I started making my way down towards the tree line. I was right out in the open. I expect the NVA to start shooting at me. My finger was on the trigger of my M16. The Kingbee had left by now and was orbiting somewhere nearby. I was sure Skau was watching this scenario playing out from above, but I had to means of telling for sure. I reached the end of the clearing and was about to

enter the tree line, when a figure came out from behind a tree. It was an American team member from the crash. We looked at each other for a moment and I was wondering if my face had the same scared look on it as his. He looked tired, scared, exhausted, his clothing was all torn up, and then, I noticed one of his legs had a splint on it. It was made from tree branches. I checked it out. He did a good job of dressing and splinting the leg. He said he broke it when the H-46 went down. I asked him if there were any other men with him. He said "No, just me." About that time, I began to wonder how I was going to get the Kingbee back to get us out. I had no radio. And then, like an angel from heaven, the Kingbee came hovering in with two McGuire Rigs dangling from the cable hoist. I said to myself, "Skau you wonderful son-of-a-bitch, you been watching us all the time." I helped the injured E-6 to the hovering chopper. His leg was in bad shape, with the help of stick as a crutch we made our way up the hill to the dangling McGuire Rigs. I helped him into the rig and got into the second one. I made sure both of our wrists were secured in the wrist straps. We were face-to-face now and starting up to the chopper.

The hoist started pulling us up to the Kingbee. The Vietnamese pilots were the best. Instead of hovering and pulling us all the way into the chopper, they start forward and up away from harm's way. This technique made it difficult for enemy soldiers to shoot at the moving chopper and the men being rescued. There we were the E-6 and I getting the ride of our lives, while the door gunner hoisted us into the Kingbee." *Ron Romancik*

Ron and the E6 returned to the safety of Phu Bai. The other Americans (2) and indigenous (3) members of the ST from Okinawa were never recovered. One of the CH46 crew members observed the helicopter burst into flames and later, he saw the charred remains of a man, assumed to be Colonel Lopez, trapped between the chopper and the ground. The Colonels remains were never recovered.

Never Forget

Just two months after Colonel Lopez was lost because of, what we believe to be a mishap with a jungle penetrator, another deadly incident happened, involving Spike Team Alabama and my best friend, Ken Cryan. Ken and I were up early on 3 May 1968. Our gear was packed and we were both ready to launch on separate missions. The previous day, SSGT John Allen and I had shared a chopper ride to our respective target areas across the border into Laos. We had each visually searched our targets and located suitable Landing Zones for our teams. John and I watched enemy tracers and 37mm anti-aircraft guns flying by the open door of the Kingbee as we approached our respective targets. This was a common occurrence in areas around the "Valley of Death" and only accented the strength of enemy forces in the area. Most men of SOG felt safer on the ground than while exposed to enemy fire while flying in the low and slow helicopters. I had often watched a Kingbee flying overhead and wondered why the enemy usually missed their shots. I was certain that I could bring one down with either automatic fire from my CAR 15 or an High Explosive round from the sawed off M-79 grenade launcher. Fortunately, all aircraft over South Vietnam were friendly, so I never had to test my theory.

The morning was a good one for a launch. The brilliant, blue sky was enhanced by only a few, puffy, blue clouds in the distance. Ken was somber as we shared breakfast in the mess hall. He was usually cheerful and outgoing, but today he ate quietly, with little to say. Noticing the extreme change in his demeanor, I asked if something was bothering him. He responded that he had a very bad feeling about today's mission. After picking up his gear, he headed off to meet with his team before launch.

About a half hour later, two Kingbee circled the camp low and landed on the FOB 1 Airstrip. Knowing this to mark the immanent launch of a team, I grabbed my weapon, walked out the camp gate and across Route 1 to the airstrip. St Alabama was already on the strip and awaited the order to board the helicopters. I shook hands with John Allen, Ken Cryan, and Paul King wishing them a safe return. Two UH1 Marine gunships (the armed escort for the insertion) arrived overhead and the order was given for ST Alabama to mount up. I waved goodbye to my friends, not knowing that this would be the last time I would see Ken alive.

ST Alabama, at that time, consisted of Staff Sergeant John Allen as One Zero, Specialist 5 Ken Cryan, as One One, PFC Paul King as the radio operator or One Two. The team also included three Nungs on today's mission. Their target was to the North of the Ashau Valley and several kilometers inside Laos. The retreating North Vietnamese, after suffering great losses in their failed Tet Offensive had run through the dreaded "Valley of Death" (Ashau) on the series of trails and roads, known as the Ho Chi Minh trail and were hiding in the surrounding mountainous jungle within the "safety" of Laos.

General Westmorland had ordered SOG to gather Intel on the positions, strength, supplies and movement of the enemy in the area, in preparation for and continuing support of Operation Delaware. This operation included the reoccupation of the Ashau Valley by the 101st Airborne Division, the 1st Calvary Division, 3d ARVN Regiment, 1st ARVN Division and the 1st ARVN Airborne Task Force. Friendly forces killed about 800 North Vietnamese, capturing huge caches of enemy weapons, food and ammunition. The operation began on 19 April and terminated on 17 May 1968.

The North Vietnamese Army had been soundly defeated in their Tet Offensive, had been chased across the borders into Laos and Cambodia. Laos and Cambodia had both declared neutrality in the war and so the US and South Vietnamese military units were barred from pursuing them across the border. This is where the secret war of SOG was fought. Our clandestine mission was to monitor enemy strength and movement, to gather other intelligence, and to snatch prisoners when we could. Enemy strength in our Area of Operation would greatly increase during April and May of 1968 as new NVA replacements arrived from the North, while retreating NVA elements escaped Operation Delaware into the jungles of Laos.

It was afternoon before the choppers returned from inserting ST Alabama. They had refueled and were ready to insert ST New Jersey into the jungles of Laos and only about a mile or two from where they had just inserted ST Alabama. I was the One Zero of ST New Jersey and Ron Zaiss was my One Two. We had selected four of our Vietnamese to accompany us on the mission. Due to the extreme danger in the Target area, I had ordered all team members to carry extra ammo and ordinance, and less food. Although the mission was scheduled for five days, my experience on previous missions told me that we would probably not be staying more than two nights.

ST New Jersey walked out the front gate and onto the landing strip. Passersby, on highway one, included both US personnel who were based up the road and indigenous, civilian and military. Some stopped to stare at this unconventional group of mixed US and Vietnamese guerillas, dressed in unmarked uniforms and painted up with catalogue paint. The team was armed to the teeth and certainly did not look too friendly. The out of the ordinary appearance of the team was further enhanced by the two, old ARVN helicopters waiting on the runway and the clouds of dust swirling up from the rotors.

Kingbee on FOB 1 Airstrip

When our gunship escorts arrived overhead, we mounted up for our trip to Laos. As we lifted off, we looked back at our friends on the airstrip. We were brothers who truly cared about each other and, if necessary, we would risk our own life to save each other. Even to this day, I would trust my life to any of these my war brothers.

The flight to the LZ lasted about an hour and the air blasting in the open doorway cooled us in the tropical heat. We wore long-sleeved jungle fatigues, which were tight at the sleeve to help protect us from the insects, leeches, and thorny vines through which we would have to pass. We had treated the fatigues by soaking them with DEET and then washing them. The DEET which remained in the fabric, helped keep the malaria infected mosquitoes away, but also made the uniforms less comfortable in the hot climate. We also smeared lanolin based leech repellant around the top of our boots, on our sleeves, and collars to keep those blood suckers off our bodies.

I had chosen an LZ of tall elephant grass on a gentle slope. The spot was just large enough for a chopper to hover above the grass, while the team jumped to the ground below. We had drawn enemy fire en route from both small arms and anti aircraft guns. As we neared the LZ, I sat in the open door and watched for any sign of the enemy, as the gunships swooped down to treetop level over the LZ. The Marine UH1 gunships did not draw any fire and I saw no other trails of activity, which would cause me to abort the mission. I told the team to ready as the ARVN H34 slipped down to a position, with its wheels only inches from the elephant grass. I scanned the area for punji stakes and seeing none, gave the order to go. The Two Nungs jumped into the tall grass and I followed. We quickly scattered to the edges of the grass, as we had practiced many times to set up a defensive perimeter. After our chopper had cleared the LZ, chopper two, carrying Ron Zaiss and the other two Vietnamese, pulled into position and the three men jumped to the ground. I regrouped the team and signaled the point man to head up the slope, into the cover and "safety" of the jungle.

After the team had moved about 25 meters into the jungle, I had Zaiss call covey with a team OK. After that, the distinctive whop-whop sounds of the choppers faded into the distance and the jungle was quiet. We remained still and listened for a few minutes to ensure that we did not have any "company" in this place. Hearing none, I instructed the point man to move slowly uphill from the LZ and to look for a suitable place for the team to spend the night. (RON) We travelled slowly and quietly for about an hour and a half before we crossed a well used enemy trail on the ridge. The brush had all been cleared and the ground was hard packed from foot traffic along the trail. We took cover and observed the trail for about fifteen minutes. I marked it on my topo map, using terrain features and my compass to plot its location. We buried a top secret listening device in the bushes adjacent trail and then crossed the trail. I had one of the Vietnamese carefully cover our tracks so that they would not be detected by enemy soldiers moving along the trail. I also had him plant a few M-14 "toe popper" mines in our back trail to let us know if we were being followed. After placing the mines, we moved out again, now down a slope, in search of a place to spend the night. We moved down and through a ravine and then up and across another ridge. I had the point man turn left to parallel the ridge and hopefully to bring us to a vantage point that perhaps would allow us to look out over our target area.

After about 15 minutes on this track, we came to a small clearing, surrounded with big trees and vines. After checking out our surroundings, I told the team to settle in for the night. Everyone knew what to do, so we set out placing Claymore mines at possible avenue of approach. We pinpointed our location on the topo map and I had Zaiss call COVEY, reporting the location of our RON.

When Zaiss got through to COVEY on the PRC 25, he learned that ST Alabama was in trouble and that my friend Ken had been shot through the thigh. The team had taken cover in a place where they could be extracted, as they were under heavy attack by the enemy.

In the distance we could hear the gunfire, the roaring of jets, and the exploding bombs being dropped in support of ST Alabama. The gunfire was so intense that ST Alabama could not be picked up that night. Gunfire was sporadic during the night and was resumed with new vigor at first light. Paul

King was hit in the head with a large caliber weapon and was killed instantly. All but one of the indigenous team members was also killed. Several attempts were made to pick up the team and the choppers were driven off by intense enemy fire. Only after One Zero, John Allen, had called in Napalm to be dropped "danger close" was he able to strap Cryan and the last wounded Nung on the jungle penetrator. He watched, as they were lifted skyward and as the murderous enemy shot them repeatedly with large caliber weapons. Their blood poured down in his face as their lives drained from them. He reported that he saw their arms and legs flailing around wildly as they were struck repeatedly by enemy fire. Apparently, the enemy never attempted to shoot the hovering helicopter, but chose to murder the defenseless, wounded men instead.

Meanwhile, ST New Jersey had broken camp and was headed uphill, parallel to the ridgeline headed for the high ground ahead. All of a sudden, all hell broke loose. We had walked unknowingly into an enemy ambush. Ahead of us, on the high ground, a machine gun fired toward us, but by some miracle, above our heads. Up the hills, to both our right and our left there was AK47 fire. I quickly accessed the situation and knew that I had to get the team out of the "kill zone" of this ambush. I ordered the team to follow me up the hill to our right flank. As I rushed uphill, the tree bark next to me exploded from the impact of the AK-47 bullets, which had been intended for me. It was then that I saw an NVA soldier dressed very similar to my teammates, but pointing an AK47 at me. I fired a burst of four rounds and saw the enemy fly backwards into the brush. I continued leading the team, while charging the hill and firing my weapon. A few grenades went off and all of a sudden, I had blood running down my face and into my left eye. I felt my face and found a wound in my left eyebrow. I moved my cravat head band down from my forehead to cover the wound and slow the flow of blood. I continued to lead the team over the ridge and into an area that was clear enough for us to be extracted. As we regrouped and took cover behind a fallen tree, I had Zaiss call for an extraction of the team.

Although we had broken free of the ambush and were relatively safe for now, we continued to receive sporadic fire and my orders were to call for extraction if we made significant enemy contact. Most of SOG's air assets were tied up trying to rescue ST Alabama, and so we waited for about an hour before a few Cobra gunships arrived on station. I shot off a pen flare and flashed a panel so the pilots could pinpoint our location. After they knew our location, Zaiss called in their rocket and mini-gun fire. The pilots reported that they were receiving gunfire from the other side of the ridge and fired some ordinance in that area as well.

During this time a couple of Slicks (Huey UH1 Helicopters) from the First Air Calvary arrived, flew in close to the ground and picked us up. I looked back from the chopper as the Cobra marked the target we had just left with white phosphorous (WP). Shortly thereafter, jet bombers dropped 500 pound bombs in the area of the WP. I gave a sigh of relief, knowing that we had narrowly escaped death, again. I noticed that I had two deep gashes on the back of my hand, which had also bled a lot. It was uncertain where they came from, but a good guess would be small pieces of shrapnel .The last word that we had received was that Ken Cryan and the other team member were alive and well, en route to the field hospital.

As we landed on the airstrip at FOB 1, we were greeted by almost all of the American personnel from the camp, as well as many of the indigenous personnel. The first man I remembered seeing was Ron Romancik. He had tears in his eyes, he ran up to me, giving me a hug, saying "Thank God you are alive." The next words out of his mouth were "Ken is dead!" I was shocked and hurt by this revelation and remembered the many good times we had shared together. Christmas Eve 1967 at the Gunfighter Saloon at CCN Da Nang, the five months as roommates at FOB 1, the Rat patrol, but now it was over.

Khanh Dohn (Cowboy) at Ken Cryan's grave in San Mateo, California

I was greeted by many others that day but I remember being welcomed home by Colonel Jack Warren, commander CCN. The Colonel had flown to the camp when he heard that two teams were in trouble. He pulled down the cravat and looked at my wound, asking if I was alright to travel. He wanted me to go to Da Nang for debriefing and to identify Ken's Body at the morgue in Da Nang. I told him I would go as soon as I got cleaned up and visited the dispensary. The Colonel told me the Kingbee were going to refuel and would return for me shortly.

I walked back into the camp with some of my friends carrying my heavy rucksack and web gear. Someone offered to load some magazines for me while I hit the shower and dispensary. This was a job that each of us did for ourselves, but this time, I was in a rush to catch that outgoing chopper, so I took him up on it.

When I arrived to my hooch, I was greeted by "Momma san" and "Babysan." These were two of the village women that worked as maids in the camp. They washed our clothes, polished our boots and made our beds. When they saw the dried blood on my face and shirt they began crying, asking if I had, killed many VC. I told them that I was ok and that I had, indeed, killed a bunch of VC (Actually NVA but they were all the same to the peaceful Catholic and Buddhist villagers).

One Two Ron Zaiss ready for a mission

After taking a shower and dressing in regular marked jungle fatigues I headed to the "Quack Shack" to have my wounds cleaned and dressed. As I entered the dispensary, I met another friend, Sgt Bruce Johnston from Seattle, Washington. Bruce cleaned my wounds, applied two stitches in my eyebrow, and a butterfly dressing on my hand. He gave me a supply of tetracycline and told me to take it for three days to prevent infection. I thanked him and went back to my hooch to pick up my weapon and web gear. The magazine pouches were all full of freshly loaded 20 round magazines and my CAR 15 had been cleaned. I had a quick beer with my friends, then took my web gear and weapon and headed for the air strip. The others were waiting and after a brief delay, we loaded into the Kingbee lifting off in a cloud of dust, and headed south toward Da Nang. We arrived over Da Nang harbor at sunset and, after landing were driven to House 22 in the open back of a Deuce and a Half.

I had not eaten since breakfast and needed some nourishment before drinking toasts to the living and the dead. At House 22, I had a wonderful steak sandwich on the heal of freshly baked French bread. It tasted great and was washed down with a very large quantity of Ba Mui Ba (33), which was my favorite Vietnamese beer. I awoke with a terrible hangover and proceeded to take the proven remedy of a salt tablet, an A.P.C, (Aspirin Phenacetin and Caffeine) and another Ba Mui Ba. The US Food and Drug administration recalled all Phenacetin containing drugs in 1983 because of its toxic and carcinogenic effects.

After a rather informal breakfast, we were picked up and driven to the US Military morgue, near the Da Nang airbase. As we entered a small office, we were met by a PFC in hospital whites. We told him what we were there for and he led us through double doors, into a very large refrigerated room.

The room was lined with stainless steel autopsy tables in neat rows, ten wide, and five deep. Each table had the body of a US military man draped over with a white sheet. The feet of each body were uncovered and there was a tag tied to a toe identifying the fallen man, and his service number and unit. It was as these brave souls were standing their last formation all "dress right dress, front and cover."

As a combat medic and a SOG recon team leader, I had seen plenty of dead and wounded, but this was somehow more shocking. Almost in unison, we removed our berets in reverence to these sons of America who had given their lives for what they believed. The PFC walked along the rows, checking the tags until he came to the one he was looking for.

In a manner unlike anything that you may have seen in a movie or on TV, the PFC grabbed the sheet and ripped it off our friend's naked body. Here was the young man who we had drank with, smoked with, and laughed with, lying dead and pale on a cold stainless steel table. He was pale because most of his blood was pumped out while he hung on that jungle penetrator. We were no experts on forensics, however: it was obvious to all present, that the terrible wound on his thigh had bled and bruised while he was still alive. The bullet holes were all the same and each was about two inches in diameter. We could peer down through the holes and see the stainless table beneath. Three or four of the holes had not bled at all, having been inflicted after he had already died. The anger and hatred against the communists' bastards stays with me to this very day. The weapon that they used to kill my defenseless friend was apparently, an antiaircraft weapon, yet they never took a shot at the chopper itself.

We signed the papers, identifying the body as Sp5 Kenneth Cryan, and left the morgue. I was taken to CCN to be debriefed about the mission, while Ron and the others were flown back to Phu Bai. During the debriefing I told the S2 officer about the loud, single shot weapon that the enemy was firing on my team and described the wounds sustained by Cryan that same day. I can still vividly see those wounds today as though I was still standing in that Da Nang morgue with my SOG brothers.

Ken Cryan is buried in Golden Gate National Cemetary in San Bruno, California. He shall always be my brother.

DEPARTMENT OF THE ARMY
HQ, 5TH SPECIAL FORCES GROUP (AIRBORNE), 1ST SPECIAL FORCES
APO San Francisco 96240

GENERAL ORDERS
NUMBER   1493

26 August 1968

AWARD OF THE BRONZE STAR MEDAL FOR HEROISM

1. TC 320. The following AWARD is announced.

PERRY, STEPHEN C RA   (SSAN   SERGEANT E5, UNITED
STATES ARMY, Headquarters and Headquarters Company (Command and Control
North), 5th Special Forces Group (Airborne), 1st Special Forces, APO 96240
Awarded: Bronze Star Medal with "V" Device (First Oak Leaf Cluster)
Date action: 22 May 1968
Theater: Republic of Vietnam
Reason: For heroism in connection with ground operations against a hostile force
in the Republic of Vietnam: Sergeant Perry distinguished himself by
heroic actions on 22 May 1968, while on a Special Forces reconnaissance
team operating deep in a denied area. The team was attacked by an
estimated enemy company. In the first few minutes of fighting, one man
was killed and seven were wounded, to include Sergeant Perry. Despite
the intense hail of enemy fire and completely ignoring the pain of his
own wounds, he helped drag the wounded into a bomb crater. Refusing
treatment for his own wounds he began administering first aid to the
other wounded, allowing them to return fire. The battle raged for an
hour and a half before helicopters were able to evacuate the wounded.
During this time, Sergeant Perry continued to move from man to man,
giving aid and comfort and firing at the enemy. Sergeant Perry's
actions were instrumental in keeping the team's position from being
overrun. His outstanding display of personal bravery and devotion to
duty are in keeping with the highest traditions of the military service and
reflect great credit upon himself, the Special Forces and the United
States Army.
Authority: By direction of the President under the provisions of Executive Order
11046, 24 August 1962.

FOR THE COMMANDER:

OFFICIAL:

T F Ryan

T. F. RYAN
1LT, AGC
Asst Adjutant

RAYMOND G. MAYER
Major, AGC
Adjutant

The Last Dance

"whoop whoop whoop, rat tat tat tat tat, boom, whoop whoop whoop"

The missions of the Special Operations Group were like a well choreographed dance. They all began in the briefing room with well dressed officers instructing the team on the peculiarities of the dance floor, discussing the special steps to be taken, and providing any and all information on the other possible participants in the production.

Following the final briefing, the team of "dancers" was assembled in the team room, and their "costumes" (uniforms) and "makeup" (camouflage face paint) were applied and later inspected by the team leaders. Camouflage paint, mosquito and leach repellants were applied in all the right places. Final checks were made of radios, automatic rifles, grenade launchers, hand grenades, assorted mines, and other explosives being carried on the mission. These weapons were very important since they would provide a significant part of the "musical score" for the dance as well as helping to protect the team when it encountered "the other side."

When all was found ready, the team was walked to the airstrip, where the musical score had already begun. The harmonious whoop, whoop, whoop of the chopper blades introduced the team to this "new dance." Once the team was loaded aboard the helicopters, they were lifted aloft for an exhilarating ride in the open cabin. The sound of the rush of hot, humid air blended nicely with the "whoop, whoop" of the rotors, as the team floated over a carpet of green for the fifty to seventy-five miles to the "dance floor." Occasionally, tracer bullets would flash by the open door, or puffs of smoke accentuated by the flash and sounds of explosions would let the team know that it was almost time to begin. These were the unfriendly signals from the "other side" that their machine guns and anti-aircraft guns were ready to do their part.

Upon arrival at the target, the team would leave the "safety" of the helicopter by either jumping from the hovering aircraft, by being lowered on a jungle penetrator, or by rappelling down a one-hundred and twenty foot rope, through the tree tops. Once all team members were on the ground, the helicopters would depart with their distinctive "whoop, whoop, whoop" fading into the distant jungle. The quiet was soon replaced with the drone of the circadid like insects and the buzzing of mosquitoes.

On May 23 1968, Spike Team (ST) Idaho launched on a mission west of the "Valley of Death" to a target deep behind enemy lines. The team on that mission consisted of only two Americans; thirty-seven year-old One Zero, Glenn Lane and his new One One, Robert D. Owen. With them were four of the indigenous members of Spike Team Idaho. The Vietnamese team leader was my friend Tu Huu Lee (Mr. Tu). The other indigenous personnel on that mission were Hung, Dong and Thuat.

Trung Si (Sergeant) Tu was a very experienced Vietnamese fighter who had served in Vietnamese military units since 1952. He served while Ngo Dinh Diem was president of South Vietnam. Mr. Tu had been fighting the communists in his country since I was still in grammar school. Tu's experience and survival during sixteen years of combat led everyone, Americans and indigenous alike, to refer to him respectfully as *MISTER Tu*, instead of just Tu. I will always remember, as though it happened yesterday when Mr. Tu took me aside to offer me the fatherly advice of a proven warrior. I had apparently proven myself worthy or Mr. Tu's friendship during one of our first firefights, while on a mission as ST Idaho's One One. Mr. Tu told me that day that whenever we got into a fire fight that I should get behind the biggest tree I could find and to do my firing from behind the tree. Mr. Tu was a very brave warrior who had survived for many years of combat. Mr. Tu was also a very wise man who was always watching out for the newcomers.

Mr. Tu was a Roman Catholic. I had enlisted in the military to help protect the South Vietnamese population's right to practice whatever religion that they desired. The population of South Vietnam was approximately 10% Roman Catholic and 70% Buddhist in 1968. After our country broke their promises to the people of South Vietnam and abandoned them to the Communist forces in 1975, all religion was suppressed and many "believers" were sent to reeducation camps or murdered because of their practice of religion.

On this day in May, Spike Team Idaho had been inserted in the sovereign country or Laos. The area of operation would continue to be "Denied" by the government of the United States for another thirty-three years. No one in the US Government was willing to admit that they had sent brave young Americans to fight and perhaps die in Laos until April 4th 2001 when the Presidential Unit Citation was issued to the Studies and Observations Group (SOG) for extraordinary heroism. At that time, the "black operations" were declassified. Because of these years of secrecy and the very nature of the operations, the accounts of what happened to ST Idaho that day are not clear. My account is that of an eye witness and does not fully agree with the official US Government account.

After the team was inserted, the Forward Air Controller (FAC) received a radio message with a team OK from Sgt Owen. Later that night word spread through FOB 1 that friendly aircraft had received further encoded communication on the emergency frequency. The team was in trouble and was moving in a particular direction being pursued by the enemy. I recall that there were several other transmissions later that night and the following morning. The seasoned members of the other spike teams gathered in small groups to discuss what was going on with our friends on ST Idaho. We were all anxious to go out and rescue Lane and the others but there was some reluctance in the S2 office about risking more lives on a Bright Light mission where only sketchy radio information was available. The Forward Air Controller spent the day trying to raise the team on the assigned frequencies with no success. Meanwhile, the warriors of FOB 1 were getting impatient with the slow response to this emergency situation. The discussions became more heated on who was most qualified to go to rescue the team. Late that day, Sgt Mike Tucker, One Zero of Spike Team Oregon was told to ready his team for a rescue attempt. Since I had worked closely with ST Idaho as One One, and was therefore familiar with Lane's tactics, I was assigned to accompany ST Oregon on the rescue mission.

Steve Perry, Mike Tucker and George Sternberg May 1968 before the ill fated Bright Light mission.

The following day a full twelve man Spike Team Oregon, including One Zero Mike Tucker, One Two George Sternberg, the author, and a young Vietnamese lieutenant that had been assigned for this mission only, launched on a Bright Light mission in hopes of rescuing our friends. The day was very hot and humid and the "dance" began as they all did. It was a relief to climb aboard the Kingbee and be cooled by the prop wash as we lifted off the airstrip. The entire camp had come out to see us off and they waved as we flew west toward the mountains of Laos.

We were inserted on the edge of a large bomb crater on a steep ridgeline. This was the last place anyone ever saw Glenn Lane and ST Idaho. The bomb had cleared a large enough area so that we were able to jump from the Kingbee as they hovered about four feet above the ground. As soon as the choppers had pulled away we were able to locate Idaho's trail, leaving the soft dirt of the crater and heading due north along a heavily forested ridge which descended into the valley below. Tucker gave the signal to follow the trail, and after I warned him of Lane's possible use of M-14 mines in his back trail, ST Oregon set out crisscrossing ST Idaho's trail for about 150 yards down the ridgeline. At one point, ST Oregon crossed the trail and climbed up on higher ground. The Point man gave the signal to freeze. After Tucker moved up to the point man's position, he called Sternberg and I to advance to his position. From the higher ground we could see into the valley below. There was a well-defined road with a red and white striped gate and a gatehouse with armed guards just a few hundred yards below us. On the other side of the road there was a hillside that was grass-covered and we observed a squad-sized element of North Vietnamese Regulars moving along a well worn trail. A few other enemy soldiers were in the area engaged in various activities. After discussing the situation, it was decided that ST Idaho must have walked down the hill right into the enemy's position. We speculated that Lane and his team had walked into a whole lot of trouble at the bottom of the hill and that they must either be dead or in captivity at some unknown location. Tucker made the decision not to repeat such a deadly mistake but to pull back to the higher ground of the crater and to call in airstrikes on the enemy positions.

The slow and silent ascent to the crater seemed to take hours as our clothing became entangled in the wait-a-minute vines and we stopped frequently to look and listen for enemy activity. When we finally reached the crater, we laid out two international orange panels on the rim of the crater and took positions in the crater facing the valley below. Several of the indigenous personnel were stationed just outside the crater to cover any enemy approach from our South. With binoculars we could make out a section of the trail but could no longer see the gate or the gatehouse since they were blocked by the trees below us. We carefully marked these enemy positions on our topo maps, and George called for air support. Special Operations Group had priority for all air resources over Southeast Asia, and whoever was near would respond to our call. The first to arrive over us was a flight of Marine F4 Phantoms. Tucker got on the radio and gave the pilots our position. After the pilots had located

127

us visually and identified our panels, Tucker gave them the coordinates of the enemy positions. We peered over the edge of the crater as the Marine bombs ripped up the distant hillside and napalm flared up in the location where we had seen the gatehouse. Secondary explosions from the area of the gatehouse indicated that the enemy had a cache of weapons and ammunition in that area.

As the bombs fell, all hell broke loose in the crater. Small arms fire erupted behind me and as I turned to look, a very scared member of ST Oregon jumped into the crater from his guard position outside the south rim. He had blood all over his right pant leg and he was white as a sheet. I calmed him down as I cut away his pant leg with my knife. He had a clean bullet wound through the flesh of his calf muscle with no apparent arterial bleeding or bone damage. Just as I was applying a battle dressing to his wound, a US made M26 hand grenade fell into the crater next to me. I yelled grenade and we all scrambled to locate it but it had become covered with the soft dirt near my feet. I yelled that it was too late and to take cover. Everyone got down on their face and covered their heads with their arms just as the grenade exploded. The bomb crater we were in was about 15 feet deep and about 25 feet across. The twelve team members had taken firing positions around the rim and all lay exposed to the blast of the grenade and its shrapnel.

Seven members of the team were injured by the shrapnel. I was closest to the grenade when it exploded and was the most seriously injured from the blast. The concussion paralyzed me from the neck down for approximately fifteen minutes. As feelings returned to my extremities I was wrenched by excruciating pain and then the tingling and numbness. I had been on eight missions before this one and had been in some pretty terrifying fire fights however, I had never felt any fear until this moment. In my crippled condition and with gunfire erupting all around us and occasional mortar and rocket rounds exploding in or near the crater, I knew that it was only a matter of time before I was killed or captured by the enemy. From the depths of my Soul I cried out to the God of my youth. I called out to Jesus Christ and promised that if He would get me out of "this one" that I would become a priest.

Sternberg had called for the team's extraction, but the helicopters were almost an hour away. The gunfire and explosions raged on but a peace had fallen on me. As I regained the use of my limbs I assessed the situation and noted that the majority of the automatic weapons fire was coming from down the hill from our South. Bullets were kicking up a lot of dirt on the south rim of the crater and Tucker and Sternberg were holding their CAR 15s high over their heads and firing on fully automatic to hinder the enemy's advance up the hill. The young Vietnamese Lieutenant lay dead in the bottom of the crater and the other indigenous personnel were also busy firing their weapons.

I grabbed my weapon and a LAW, and climbed up the west side of the crater. The area was covered with some brush and some small trees which had been damaged when the bomb crater was formed. The Vietnamese whose leg I had bandaged followed after me and stayed close by me like my latest best friend. Looking down the hill to the south I could see a group of enemy soldiers climbing up the steep hill toward the crater. I armed the LAW and fired it down the hill. The horrific explosion literally vaporized the enemy soldiers and temporarily stopped further advance from the south. I could hear both machine gun and mortar fire coming from up the hill to the west of our position but could not see the enemy because of the dense jungle that covered that hillside. A mortar round exploded nearby and I felt searing pain in the back of my left thigh as shrapnel ripped through my flesh.

Then I heard the "angels", "whoop, whoop, whoop" approaching from the east. Noting that the clump of damaged trees on the west rim of the crater may cause a problem for the extraction, I tied a Claymore Mine to the center of the bunch and crawled back into the crater to detonate it. The explosion took the trees down and left the best place for a helicopter to hover. As the choppers came into view, Tucker instructed me to take a few of the other wounded team members and to get aboard the first chopper. With my new "best friend" with the wounded leg at my side, we loaded three other wounded indigenous soldiers on the Kingbee. As the helicopter lifted off, bullets ripped through the fuselage and tracers lit up the air around us. The door gunner on the Kingbee was busy firing the thirty caliber machine gun in an attempt to suppress the ground fire while we tossed out hand grenades on the enemy.

As we gained altitude we could see enemy firing positions all around the bomb crater and piles of bodies to the south and east of the crater. The jets continued to strafe the area with their 20mm guns and a few Cobra gunships fired both High Explosive and White Phosphorous rockets into the hillside to the direct west of the crater. We could see our tiny band of brothers pinned down in that crater with Hell itself closing in around them. As we pulled away we watched the second Kingbee swoop down to extract the rest of the team. As our helicopter crossed the ridgeline to the east we lost sight of the crater but observed a platoon-sized element in formation moving along the dirt road in the direction of the action. Later, we were told that the Forward Air Controller had estimated the size of the enemy element which had our twelve men pinned down at about 1000. With the odds like they were it was truly a miracle that we escaped with only seven injured and one killed.

The excitement for the day had not yet ended. As we approached the FOB 1 airstrip the Vietnamese Crew Chief announced "fini petrol." The Kingbee had taken many bullets during our extraction and apparently the fuel tanks had been leaking gas all the way home. The Kingbee pilots were the best in the business and ours autorotated the old bird for a hard landing on the airstrip. I was helped to a waiting ambulance by a few of the crowd awaiting our return. I was rushed off to the Marine Corps field hospital in Phu Bai, where my wounds were cleaned and debrided. The following day I was loaded into a C130 and flown to Da Nang where I was transferred by ambulance to an Army tent hospital on the beach near Marble Mountain.

For the next thirty days, I lay in a bed in that tent hospital. My bandages were changed once a day and I was given injections of penicillin and streptomycin every four hours. Before long, the injection sites in my buttocks were more painful than the wounds themselves. Being a trained medic I knew full well that the Standard Operating Procedure for gunshot or shrapnel wounds was to clean and debride them followed by three days of penicillin and streptomycin. After three days, showing no signs of infection, the wounds should have been sutured closed. In my case it was just more injections and no sutures. When I attempted to question the nurse about my treatment, I was given some snarky "what the hell do you know" kind of an answer. I did not want to be a bother since there were many in my "tent" that were in much worse shape than I. After thirty days of negligence in this tent, having never seen a doctor and getting very weary of the snarky nurses and their injections, I got on a radio and called the SOG FOB down the road. Less than an hour later an SFC came into my "tent" and escorted me back to the FOB. I had only the blue hospital pajamas that I was wearing and had a difficult time walking due to my injuries. My rescuer took me directly to the club at the FOB and ordered me a drink. Within a few minutes I was approached by an officer and told that I had to leave because the hospital blue pajamas were not allowed in the club. My new SFC friend explained who I was and why I was here and the officer relented, bought a few rounds and eventually escorted me to the dispensary.

The senior medic examined my wounds and told me that they had granulated to the point that they could not be sutured and that the resultant scars would be a lot larger than if they would have been properly treated. He suggested that I hang out on the beach in front of the camp for a few weeks, noting that the salt water would help the healing along. And so, for about two weeks in July of 1968 I spent my days lying on the beach in Vietnam before returning to Phu Bai. The tent hospital was never told that I was leaving, nor where I went. As incompetent as they seemed at that hospital, I am certain that they never missed me.

I returned to Phu Bai sometime in July 1968 still limping and hunched over from my wounds. I was called to the office almost immediately and told that I was needed to take my team on an important mission. I told the Sergeant Major that I was not capable of leading a mission at the time due to my injuries and he got pissed and removed me as One Zero of New Jersey and assigned me to help in the dispensary. I learned soon thereafter that my friend Bert Merriman had been hit bad and had possibly lost his leg while on a mission with Project Delta. I was told that he had been evacuated to the United States but I had no way to confirm the reports.

Discouraged by my injuries, the slow recovery and the loss of my many friends, I decided to apply for an early out to return to college. My request was granted and I was scheduled to leave Vietnam on 23 August 1968. During my last month in the country I was reunited with Mike Tucker and George Sternberg who were also recovering from their wounds. Another surprise reunion was with my friend Ha who was the ST Idaho point man who had acted as our point man on ST Oregon for the Bright Light mission. He was recovering from his wounds of that "last dance" as well. He had counted 97 bullet and shrapnel wounds, and although his skin had healed, he was in pretty sorry shape after a month in the Vietnamese hospital.

I had some good times with Tucker and Sternberg and my other friends in FOB 1 for my last month in the country and departed the FOB 1 airstrip by Kingbee on August 20, 1968. In Da Nang I was taken to SOG headquarters and debriefed. I was told, as I was when I arrived, that what I did while assigned to SOG would be classified Top Secret forever. From Da Nang I was flown to Saigon and processed for flight back to the United States. On 23 August 1968 I climbed on a big-assed bird and headed west to the land that I loved and to the family I had left behind a year before. My seventeen hour flight home made stops in Australia and Hawaii and eventually landed in Oakland, California. I was processed out of the Army and left for Huntington Beach the following day. En Route, I was confronted by some long haired hippi dinks at the San Francisco airport that shouted obscenities and called me baby killer. What had happened to my country while I was away?

Warnings for Today!

In the words of my cousin Mike (Mouse) McGhie, *"every grunt knows that we won the war in Vietnam. We kicked their ass from the Mekong Delta to the DMZ. In every major battle they were soundly defeated."* Mike is disabled from wounds he received in Vietnam while serving with the 1st Calvary. He was raised in Las Vegas, Nevada by his parents Lynn and Margaret McGhie. Mike also enlisted because he believed in "Truth, Justice, and the American Way." It is how we were raised!

After the Communists suffered a great defeat in the Tet offensive of 1968 and the bombings of Hanoi and Haipong had shaken North Vietnam to its core, the war was all but over. However, back home on the streets of America and in our political chambers we were losing the final battle.

Our politicians were ready to throw in the towel, and public opinion at home was in the tank. Walter Cronkite had already proclaimed the war lost and so the Paris Peace talks began in January 1969.

After four years of deliberations in Paris, the "Peace" accord was signed in January of 1973. The major terms included a cease fire, withdrawal of American forces and the return of all prisoners held "in North Vietnam." In March of 1973 the last of the American troops left South Vietnam but the North Vietnamese soldiers remained in battle position in the South. Our politicians really know how to make a BAD deal!

Our POWs were returned from the POW camps in North Vietnam. However: not one American was returned from captivity in Laos of Cambodia. Many of these POWs were the heroes of SOG.

So, if we won, how did we lose?

In my opinion, we lost because we did not all stand United for "Truth, Justice and the American Way." The kryptonite that brought us to our knees was our loss of honor and dignity as the greatest nation on earth.

Rare acts of horrific brutality during the war were spotlighted on the evening news. Young soldiers returning from the war in Vietnam were dishonored in the streets by their fellow Americans. Facing rejection at home, many of the war's heroes self-medicated with alcohol or drugs, and our nation got weaker. Tens of thousands of our Nation's Vietnam veterans suffer from Post Vietnam Syndrome (now PTSD) and many tens of thousands of those are incarcerated.

In June of 1973, Congress passed the Case-Church Amendment which prohibited and further military involvement in Vietnam and thus the Communists knew that they had won.

Our politicians, in their rush to get us out of Vietnam left behind the POWs in Laos and broke all promises to the people of South Vietnam for financial aid. The armies of South Vietnam literally ran out of ammunition trying to defend their land from the Communists aggressors. Finally, in 1975 the hordes of the North Vietnam Army overran the South while the US abandoned its embassy and rescued a small number of our Vietnamese friends. Later, we watched on our TV sets as thousands of "boat people" attempted to escape the tyranny and oppression which was now Vietnam.

Iraq and Afghanistan

Let us not repeat the horrible mistakes of the Vietnam War. Let us honor our returning troops and provide them with what they need to merge back into our society.

We have already seen all the dirt that the media could muster concerning Abu Ghraib and Guantanamo Bay. Let us not forget that war is Hell and that there may be isolated acts that we do not approve of. The fact remains that our country chose to engage in battles to "Free the Oppressed" in Iraq and to destroy the terrorist networks that wish us harm. Our soldiers are honorable and battle for justice. We, in turn, need to support and honor *them*.

We have already seen and heard the cries for withdraw and the politician's pledges to be out of Iraq and Afghanistan by certain dates. This is exactly what we did with the Paris Peace talks, by fully disclosing our intentions to the enemy. Let us not waste American lives on political folly. Let us not succumb to the green kryptonite which will eventually kill our Nation. Let us work until the job is done and then support the fledgling governments as friends and allies.

Heed this last stanza of the Star Spangled Banner and note how far we have wandered as a Nation since it was first written in 1814.

> *O, thus be it ever when freemen shall stand,*
> *Between their loved home and the war's desolation!*
> *Blest with victory and peace, may the heav'n-rescued land*
> *Praise the Power that hath made and preserved us a nation!*
> *Then conquer we must, when our cause. it is just,*
> *And this be our motto: "In God is our trust"*
> *And the star-spangled banner in triumph shall wave*
> *O'er the land of the free and the home of the brave!*

Let us refocus our moral compass to ensure that "Truth, Justice and the American Way" prevail. We are indeed One Nation, Under God, and without God, we are doomed as a Nation and as a people.

God Bless America.

Ron Zaiss photo

Steve Perry with the refreshments 1968

GLOSSARY

A-1E Skyraider....a fixed wing, radial engine aircraft that could provide close   support for teams on the ground. Code name HOBO.

AO....area of operation

APC...."All Purpose Capsule" Aspirin, Phenacetin and Caffeine in widespread use during the 60s later banned due to ill effects of Phenacetin.

Arc Light....the code name for bombings from B52s.

AK 47....primary weapon of the North Vietnamese, produced in China and Russia it fired 7.62mm ammunition.

Blackbird....top secret aircraft(C130s and C123) usually flown by Asian pilots in civilian clothing. The black camouflaged paint on the exterior separated them from similar aircraft during the Vietnam war.

Bright Light....Code name for a rescue mission of downed pilots, POWs or other SOG teams in trouble.

CAR-15....A COLT Automatic Rifle which served as the primary weapon of the SOG Spike teams that fired 5.56mm ammunition. The Car-15 had a shorter barrel, an expandable stock and a higher rate of fire than the M-16 carried by conventional US forces.

C&C....Command and Control. Used as designation of SOG area of operation when it included North, Central or South. C&C North worked the I Corps area of Vietnam and was headquartered in Da Nang.

CCN....Command and Control North

CID....Central Intelligence Division

CIDG....Civilian Irregular Defense Group

Claymore Mine....a defensive anti personnel mine that consisted of one and one half pounds of C-4 in a plastic case with about 700 ball bearings that would be shot out in a deadly arc when the device was detonated.

CMB....Combat Medical Badge

CO....Commanding officer

Covey....Code name and call sign of US Airforce Forward Air Controllers for SOG. They provided a necessary commo link as well as eyes in the sky as a team was inserted or needed assistance directing air strikes against the enemy.

DMZ....Demilitarized Zone, the strip of land at the 17th parallel which separated North and South Vietnam..

E&E....Escape and Evade

Eldest Son....was A Top Secret project of modifying NVA ammunition so that it would explode within the weapon when fired. This deadly ammunition was "planted" in NVA supply dumps or along enemy supply routes by SOG teams.

FOB....Forward Operational Base, location designated by number 1, 2, 3 or 4.

FOB 1....SOG base near the villages of Phu Luong and Phu Bai.

FOB 3....SOG base outside the Marine wire at Khe Sanh.

FOB 4....SOG base, on the beach, near Da Nang

HF....**Hatchet Force**.... a platoon or company sized SOG element used in larger operations.

Ho Chi Minh Trail....a road and foot trail complex leading from North Vietnam to South Vietnam through the "neutral" countries of Laos and Cambodia.

Hooch….a house, hut or shack in which someone lives.

House 22…. an old French villa at 22 Lei Loi street, Danang used a safe house by CCN.

Indig….indigenous SOG personnel. Nungs, Vietnamese, Montagnard and Cambodian.

Jolly Green Giant….Sikorsky helicopter was a heavy, long range helicopter.

Kingbee….Sikorsky H-34 helicopter. These older helicopters were flown by highly skilled Vietnamese pilots and were the main source of transportation for SOG spike teams.

LAW….M-72 light anti tank weapons consisted of a single use fiberglass tube which fired a 66mm high explosive rocket.

LZ….Landing Zone, or at least a big enough break in the trees where a team could be lifted out of the jungle on a jungle penetrator of McGuire rig.

M-79….40mm grenade launcher

MACV….Military Assistance Command Vietnam

MIA….Missing In Action

MOS…. A United States military occupation code, or a Military Occupational Specialty code.

Montagnard….French word for mountain people. Indigenous clans that lived in the mountains of Southeast Asia…also referred to as **Yards**

MSG….Master Sergeant, E8 military pay grade

NCO….Non Commissioned Officer

Nungs…. The descendants of those who had migrated to South Vietnam from China. These men were Recruited as mercenaries to serve on SOG teams.

NVA....The army and soldiers of North Vietnam.

O2....see A1E Skyraider

One One....the American who was second in command on a SOG spike team.

One Two.... The American who was the radio operator on the SOG spike team.

One Zero....the American team leader on a SOG spike team

PETN....(chemical compound), a highly explosive organic compound belonging to the same chemical family as nitroglycerin and nitrocellulose.

PFC....Private First Class, E3 military pay grade.

Prairie Fire.... The code name for operations within Laos

Prairie Fire Emergency....The code name for a SOG team in trouble. If declared by the team, all US air resources were diverted from their missions to assist the team on the ground.

PRC 25....FM receiver/transmitter, the primary field radio during the Vietnam war.

PX....post exchange or store.

RON....Remain over night

S2....the base security office or officer.

SF....US Special Forces

SFC....Sergeant First Class, E7 military pay grade

Slicks....UH-1 helicopter without exterior rocket pods or mini guns mounted on the sides (Slick) used to transport troops and supplies.

SMG....sergeant major also CSM for command sergeant major, E9 military pay grade is the senior enlisted , non commisioned rank.

Smoke....grenades that emitted various colors of smoke used to mark a target or the location of a ST in the jungle.

SOG.... Surveillance and Observation Group or Studies and Operations Group or Special Operations Group

Spike Team or ST....a SOG recon team later designated RT.

SSG....Staff Sergeant

Tet....Chinese new year

Toe Popper....an anti personnel mine carried by SOG teams. The device was housed in plastic and about the size of a small can of tuna. If stepped on by an enemy combatant it would incapacitate the enemy by blowing off a few toes or perhaps a foot.

URC-10....ultra high frequency emergency radio and homing beacon carried by all Americans on SOG Spike Teams.

VC....Viet Cong. South Vietnamese combatants opposed to the government of South Vietnam. VC was also used commonly to designate any enemy combatant including the regular NVA soldiers encountered by SOG teams.

VR....Visual Reconnaissance.

XO....Executive Officer, second in command in a US military base or unit.